Essex County Council

D1362539

www.booksattransworld.co.uk

30130 145267943

AUDREY EYTON
the F2 cookbook

Recipes in association with Roz Denny

Scientific consultant: Dr Alison Stephen

BANTAM PRESS

LONDON · TORONTO · SYDNEY · AUCKLAND · JOHANNESBURG

TRANSWORLD PUBLISHERS

61-63 Uxbridge Road, London W5 5SA

a division of The Random House Group Ltd

RANDOM HOUSE AUSTRALIA (PTY) LTD

20 Alfred Street, Milsons Point, Sydney,

New South Wales 2061, Australia

RANDOM HOUSE NEW ZEALAND LTD

18 Poland Road, Glenfield, Auckland 10, New Zealand

RANDOM HOUSE SOUTH AFRICA (PTY) LTD

Isle of Houghton, Corner of Boundary Road & Carse O'Gowrie,

Houghton 2198, South Africa

Published 2006 by Bantam Press

a division of Transworld Publishers

A catalogue record for this book is available
from the British Library.
ISBN 9780593055304 (from Jan 07)
ISBN 0593055306

Typesetting: Falcon Oast Graphic Art Ltd

Design: Phil Lord/Fiona Andreanelli

Photography: Steve Baxter

Food stylist: Caroline Marson

Printed in Germany

1 3 5 7 9 10 8 6 4 2

Papers used by Transworld Publishers are natural, recyclable products made
from wood grown in sustainable forests. The manufacturing processes
conform to the environmental regulations of the country of origin.

CONTENTS

INTRODUCTION

THE RECIPES IN *The F2 Cookbook* are designed to do very much more than simply liven up your menus with lots of tasty new dishes. This they will certainly do. But at the same time they will be feeding millions of hidden helpers in your digestive system, which have it in their power to rejuvenate your inner health.

F2 recipes, which form part of the F2 eat-yourself-slim-and-fit formula, can play a major part in protecting you and your family against cancers, heart disease, diabetes and other major health threats. These are feel-good, get-fit recipes for positive well-being.

Today, awareness is rapidly growing among the health-conscious of the key role played by good bacteria in powering our immune systems. This isn't just another fleeting fad. It is soundly based on science – serious science from the most respected centres of cutting-edge research.

Remarkable though this sounds, bacteria wars are going on inside my colon and inside your colon as I write. On one side are colonies of bad bacteria-producing substances now strongly implicated in causing cancer. They have become prime suspects behind many other diseases too. On the other side are colonies of good bacteria, producing substances now known to actively protect us against such ailments.

Which bacteria survive, thrive, increase and overwhelm the opposition depends more than anything else on the kind of meals we eat. It isn't enough just to swig down probiotic milk drinks. The good bacteria these provide won't survive long without the regular supplies of fuel they need to keep them alive. All the recipes in this book are packed full of the most effective foods to feed the good bacteria naturally present in your body, as well as any good bacteria you might add. Introducing as many of these recipes as possible as often as possible into your at-home eating is one of the best things you can do for your body.

Look what's going on inside your colon on a typical British high-protein low-fibre diet!

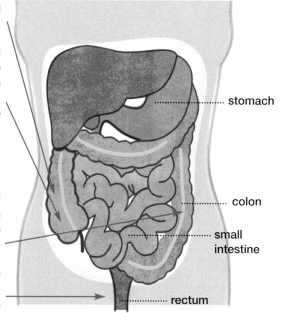

Lacking sufficient fibre to feed them, 'good bacteria' produce only a small quantity of protective anti-cancer agents.

Fed mainly on animal protein, 'bad bacteria' thrive here producing a large quantity of ammonia and nitrogen compounds suspected of causing cancer. Substances in red and processed meats are particularly highly suspect.

In the high powered 'drying machine' on this side of the colon, waste-matter, already low in volume, becomes dryer, firmer and resistant to onward movement. Food residues, high in carcinogens, linger in dangerous contact with the gut wall for days.

It takes from three days to more than a week for all the waste-matter from food consumed to be expelled in the faeces.

stomach

colon

small intestine

rectum

There are two very good reasons why focusing on bacteria balance is more important now than ever before.

- **The modern Western diet is bad-bacteria friendly.** Today we eat more animal products than did our predecessors. Among these, red meat and processed meats such as bacon, ham, sausages, burgers and deli meats are known to be the foods that fuel bad bacteria, allowing them to predominate. At the same time we eat less fibre-rich plant-based food than almost any society in history. These are the only foods that can make good bacteria flourish. It is no accident that our most serious health threats and the major causes of

Now see what's going on inside on a fibre-rich plant-based diet.

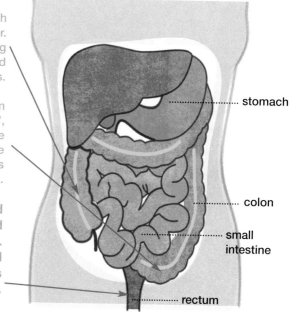

'Good bacteria' feed on fibre which stimulates them to increase in number. In doing so they *reduce* cancer-causing substances such as ammonia and *increase* protective anti-cancer agents.

Bulked and diluted by water held in undigested fibre and in 'good bacteria', waste-matter is speeded through the colon. Cancer-causing substances are not allowed to linger in dangerous contact with the gut wall.

Waste-matter is expelled effortlessly, usually within one and a half days of food being eaten. Some calories are expelled undigested, giving a weight loss advantage.

stomach

colon

small intestine

rectum

premature death in the twenty-first century were rare until we changed our diets during the second half of the last century.

- **Modern Western lifestyles make us more vulnerable to bad bacteria.** We travel, exposing ourselves to bacterial strains to which local populations have adapted but we have not. We take drugs and antibiotics, which kill off good bacteria as well as bad – leaving us vulnerable to invasion by more bad bacteria. Paradoxically, even our high standards of hygiene prevent us from building up tolerance to bad bacteria and leave us more vulnerable to attack.

Those who have lost weight on the F2 Diet will already have experienced the feeling of rejuvenation and well-being that comes from a good-bacteria-friendly high-fibre diet. The recipes in this book will help them to continue this much healthier way of eating.

Newcomers to F2 will become more aware of the 2 big Fs – the master key to good nutrition – as they explore the tips and recipes on the following pages.

F for fibre . . . the foremost food for health and weight loss

High-fibre diets offer not only the healthiest way to lose weight but the fastest too. The fibre consumed by good bacteria is not fully utilized by the body to add to or maintain surplus fat. The fibre that bacteria can't break down speeds up the passage of gut contents, increasing the number of calories lost from the body in faeces. So, on say a typical 1,500-calorie high-fibre slimming diet, you experience the speed of weight loss that could only be achieved on other diets by cutting calories by a further 150 or more. And fibre-rich meals have unique stomach-filling power that takes the hunger out of dieting. They also take care of 'the GI factor', helping to keep blood-sugar levels on a healthily even keel.

F for fats . . . the most fattening and health-threatening foods

As well as boosting the fibre, these F2 recipes help to reduce the health-threatening fat in your diet. All fats are fattening – twice as fattening as any other foods, including sugar. But some fats – the saturated fats richly present in many dairy foods and meat products, and the hydrogenated fats in ready-mades such as biscuits, cakes and crisps and some margarines – have long been rated the single greatest health risk in the Western diet. A truly vast quantity of evidence links them with heart disease and a rapidly growing volume of research strongly implicates them in causing cancers.

The F2 recipes in this book steer you towards the good fats, which can benefit health. These are the liquid polyunsaturated and monounsaturated vegetable oils. But even these are used – as they should be – with moderation. All the recipes in this book are restrained in their use of fats, making them relatively low in calories, and many are ideal for those who want to shed weight.

Everyone, whether young or old, overweight or slim, will benefit from introducing recipes from this book into their everyday eating. Read on and cook up a slim, fit future for you and yours.

SALT: we have left you to determine the quantity of salt you choose to use in these recipes, but we recommend that you limit salt as much as possible and aim to keep to no more than 6 grams per day. Salt will not affect your weight but is believed to be a cause of high blood pressure and strokes.

Building up your top task force

THE RECIPES IN this section are designed to delight more than your taste buds. They also provide superfood for superbacteria – your top task force of hidden helpers. There are many different strains of good (as well as bad) bacteria in our colons, among which a strain called bifidobacteria has become a major focus of scientific interest. These bacteria play a key role in beneficial bio-action, strengthening your immune system and killing off bad bacteria. Think of them as your own inner SAS task force!

Bifidobacteria are pretty picky eaters and thrive on substances called oligosaccharides, which form part of the dietary fibre only in certain specific foods. Fortunately these include one of the most ubiquitous of all foods, onions, along with the onion 'relatives', leeks and shallots. Garlic, too, is rich in oligosaccharides but, because of its highly pungent flavour, tends to be eaten in too small a quantity to be of much value in this respect.

The other superbacteria-fuelling foods are a some-what surprising assortment – asparagus, artichokes and chicory, would you believe! But all are rich in oligosaccharides, the special ingredient (believed to account for protective power in mother's milk) that fuels those very special health protectors.

We hope the recipes in this section will tempt you to eat and enjoy more of all these foods. You couldn't do anything better for your health.

THE ONION HEALTH SQUAD

Onions
Leeks
Shallots

WE'RE ALWAYS TOLD it pays to know your onions, but now we know why. When it comes to feeding your top inner task force, you can't have too much of this particular good thing – onions, and their relatives, shallots and leeks. The recipes in this section are designed to get you peeling and slicing to pamper your bifidobacteria and prove that dishes that do you good really can taste good as well.

Onions – well worth the tears

Onions already feature in so many favourite dishes, but make even more of them, and their health benefits, with these moreish meals and tips.

Cook's notes

Onions vary in strength and flavour according to the variety and season. Whatever the style of dish or recipe, chances are there's an onion to suit. Large Spanish onions are good all-rounders. They are of medium strength and quite juicy. Medium-size English and Egyptian onions are much stronger. In the summer you might find the American sweet white Vidalia or Chilean Oso onions perfect sliced in salads. Italian red onions, sold all year round, are fast becoming de rigueur for keen cooks because their gentler flavour and lovely ruby colour makes them so versatile. They are available in all sizes. Pickling onions are not only very strong in flavour, they also have lower water content, so pickle well. These are not to be confused with baby 'pearl' onions, which can be popped directly into casseroles.

In cooked dishes, onions are nicest if cooked fully so that they taste naturally sweet without a hint of bitterness. This can be achieved by gentle cooking at the start in a covered pan, known by chefs as 'sweating'. For raw onions, it is a good idea to lessen the strength by soaking in one or two changes of cold water.

Always squeeze onions gently when purchasing: they should feel firm. Slightly soft ones are beginning to turn mushy. Store onions in a cool dry place, out of direct sunlight. However, if they do start to sprout, don't waste the pretty green tops – snip them like spring onions.

Sweet and Sour Onions

These are so versatile as the base for a main meal (such as grilled chicken) or as a flavourful topping for jacket potatoes, roasted butternut squash or sliced and barbecued sweet potato. In the winter months, sprinkle with some healthy juicy pomegranate seeds and a few chopped walnuts; in summer, try them with a small handful of redcurrants to go with grilled mackerel.

SERVES 4
- 3–4 large red or 2 Spanish onions
- 1 tbsp olive or vegetable oil
- leaves from 2 sprigs fresh thyme
- 3–4 tbsp red wine vinegar
- 2 tbsp clear honey
- 200ml/7fl oz stock
- sea salt and freshly ground black pepper

OPTIONAL
- seeds from half pomegranate or 150g/5oz fresh redcurrants
- 2 tbsp chopped walnuts
- 2 tbsp chopped fresh parsley

1 Peel the onions, keeping the root ends intact, although they can be lightly trimmed. Cut into eights for wedges. Toss gently in a bowl with the oil. Heat a large non-stick shallow saucepan or deep frying pan and tip in the onions in a single layer.

2 Cook on a medium heat for about 10 minutes, shaking the pan occasionally, and when lightly browned turn the onions, keeping them as intact as possible. Then turn again, sprinkle with the thyme and seasoning and cook for another 5 minutes.

3 Stir in the vinegar and cook until reduced, then add the honey and stock. Cook on a low heat for a further 10 minutes until the onions are softened but still have a good bite. Garnish with pomegranate seeds or redcurrants, the walnuts and parsley as liked.

Cook's note: You could make a double-size batch and freeze leftovers in portions. These sweet and sour onions taste even better reheated.

Onion, Red Bean and Tomato Soup

This recipe has all the reds – onions, beans and tomatoes. This is good comfort food, a main-meal soup with oligosaccharide-rich onions and fibre-rich kidney beans. To give the soup a creamy texture, purée or mash half the beans. Nice served with a small dollop of reduced-fat crème fraîche or low-fat natural yogurt per bowl and a small crusty wholemeal roll on the side.

SERVES 4

- 2 red onions, chopped
- 2 tbsp olive or sunflower oil
- 2 tbsp balsamic or red wine vinegar
- 400g can chopped tomatoes
- 1 tsp dried oregano
- 410g can red kidney beans, drained
- 300ml/½ pint water
- 1–2 tbsp barbecue-style sauce (e.g. HP) or a few dashes Worcestershire sauce
- sea salt and freshly ground black pepper

1 Sauté the onion in a large saucepan with the oil and 2–3 tbsp water for about 5 minutes until softened.

2 Stir in the vinegar and cook for 1 minute until evaporated. Add the tomatoes, seasoning and oregano. Bring to the boil then simmer for 10 minutes until reduced slightly.

3 Blitz half the beans in a food processor if you want a creamy texture, or crush with a potato masher or fork. Add all the beans to the pan with the water, and sauce to taste. Return to a simmer for 5 minutes then serve.

Slimmer's tip: Adding some water to the oil at the start of the recipe helps moisten the onions without the risk of them burning, but for a low-fat variation you can omit the oil altogether and cook the onion gently in a covered pan with about 4–5 tbsp water until softened.

Onion and Potato Boulangère

This is an almost fat-free potato and onion bake, similar to a potato Lyonnaise (see cook's note below) but made with fat-free stock instead of all that fattening, saturated-fat-packed cream. It makes a good filling main meal and can be served with steamed green cabbage or green beans. Use slightly waxy potatoes.

SERVES 2
- 1 large or 2 medium potatoes, such as Maris Piper or King Edwards
- 1 large Spanish onion
- 1 fat clove garlic, chopped, optional
- 1 tbsp chopped fresh rosemary or thyme leaves
- 500ml/18fl oz hot stock
- 1 tbsp low-fat spread, melted, optional
- a little chopped fresh parsley, to serve
- sea salt and freshly ground black pepper

1 Scrub the potatoes; no need to peel. Slice them as thinly as possible. This can be done in a food processor fitted with a slicing blade or by hand using a mandolin or Japanese vegetable slicer. If you have none of these, then use your sharpest knife possible. The slices do need to be thin.

2 Slice the onion thinly into rings, or halve and slice if that is easier. Heat the oven to 180°C/gas 4. Mix the garlic, if using, with a little salt so it sprinkles more easily.

3 Layer the potatoes and onions into a medium-size baking dish, sprinkling in between with the garlic, salt, pepper and rosemary. Pour over the stock, making sure it seeps between the layers. If you want a golden top, brush with the melted low-fat spread. Place the dish in a roasting pan and bake for about 1 hour until the top is crisp, the stock absorbed and the potato soft. Cool for 10 minutes or so before serving.

Cook's note: You could use skimmed or semi-skimmed milk instead of stock to make a light potato Lyonnaise.

Panzanella – Italian Tomato, Onion and Bread Salad

Just as we soak bread in soft red fruits for summer pudding, so the Italians like to layer tomatoes with country-style bread so the juices soak in and make a delicious salad. Choose fibre-rich wholemeal bread and add thinly sliced sweet summer onions and leaves of fresh basil to make it wonderfully healthy. Also good made with shallots.

SERVES 2

- 1 large sweet white or red onion, about 200g/7oz
- 2 thick slices crusty wholemeal bread
- 2 large ripe beef tomatoes
- 1 tbsp olive oil
- 1–2 tbsp red wine or balsamic vinegar
- leaves from 1 large sprig fresh basil
- sea salt and freshly ground black pepper

1 Thinly slice the onion and soak in cold water to cover for 10–15 minutes. Drain and pat dry.

2 Dunk the bread quickly in another bowl of cold water then squeeze dry without breaking up the slices. Place in the base of a salad dish.

3 Slice the tomato thinly. Whisk together the oil, vinegar and seasoning as a dressing.

4 Layer the onions and tomatoes over the bread, sprinkling the dressing and seasoning in between. Tear the basil leaves into pieces and tuck in between the onions and tomatoes. Cover and chill 2–4 hours before serving.

Slimmer's tip: You can omit the oil and increase the vinegar by 1 tbsp. The salad can be made up to 24 hours ahead.

Eat-a-lotta-leeks!

Leeks, like onions, are food of the gods for superbacteria. Lucky for us they are one of the most versatile of vegetables, hot or cold. Perfect for soups or with pasta, they also make a simple, stylish starter when blanched (lightly cooked), cooled, tossed in a lemony vinaigrette dressing and topped with chopped parsley and hard-boiled egg. Here are just a few of the many ways to enjoy them all year round.

Cook's notes
Don't waste the dark green end of leeks – they add a delicate colour to dishes. Simply trim the top and roots, then slice to use. Leeks, when sold loose, may need a thorough swishing in cold water – you may have to split them first to the centre and shake vigorously in cold water to remove any stubborn soil.

Pea and Leek Vichyssoise

This recipe is crammed full of fibre-rich peas as well as superbacteria-feeding leeks – a powerful partnership for positive health. A great classic soup, Vichyssoise can be puréed to a wonderful low-fat creaminess. Even better, as an all-season soup it can be served hot for winter or chilled for summer. Why not make a lot while you're about it? The leftover soup freezes well.

SERVES 4

- 4 large leeks, lightly trimmed and thinly sliced
- 1 medium potato (about 250g/9oz), scrubbed and chopped
- 2 tbsp olive or sunflower oil
- leaves from 1 sprig fresh thyme
- 454g pack frozen peas, thawed
- 1.5 litres/2½ pints vegetable stock, made with a cube
- 1–2 tbsp fresh lemon juice
- sea salt and freshly ground black pepper

1 Put the leeks and potatoes into a large saucepan and mix well with the oil. Add a third of a mug of water and the thyme and heat until sizzling. Cover and cook gently to sweat for 10 minutes.

2 Stir in the peas, stock and a little seasoning. Bring to the boil, then simmer for 10 minutes. Strain the liquid into a jug and blitz the cooked vegetables with a hand-held electric blender or in a food processor until really creamy, gradually adding the hot liquid back.

3 If serving hot, return to the saucepan and reheat gently. If serving cold, then cool and chill. Check seasoning, adding lemon juice to taste.

Slimmer's tip: For a low-fat variation, omit the oil and sweat vegetables in half a mug of water, in step 1.

Haddock and Leek Chowder

Chowders are ideal as light one-pot meals. No need to pre-cook the fish, simply cut it into small chunks and drop into the simmering soup a few minutes before serving. You could substitute peeled prawns for the fish, if you like, but ensure they are first thawed if using from frozen.

SERVES 2
- 1 tbsp olive or sunflower oil
- 1 medium potato (250g/9oz), scrubbed and chopped
- 2 medium leeks (250g/9oz), lightly trimmed and thinly sliced
- 250ml/9fl oz fish or vegetable stock, made with a cube
- leaves from 1 sprig fresh thyme
- 250ml/9fl oz skimmed milk
- 200g/7oz fillet smoked haddock or cod, skinned and chopped
- 1–2 tsp coarse grain mustard, optional
- 2 tsp fresh lemon juice
- sea salt and freshly ground black pepper

1 Heat the oil in a large non-stick saucepan and sauté the potato for 2 minutes until light golden. Stir in the leeks with half the stock and the thyme. Bring to the boil, then cover and cook gently for 5 minutes.

2 Uncover and add the remaining stock and all the milk. Bring to the boil then simmer for 10 minutes until the potato is very soft. Drop in the chopped fish and add seasoning to taste.

3 Continue to cook for 5 minutes then add the mustard, if liked, and lemon juice to taste. Check the seasoning and serve.

Slimmer's tip: For a low-fat variation, omit the oil and simply simmer the potato with the leeks in the stock.

Leek, Courgette and Quark Bake

Quark is a fat-free skimmed-milk soft cheese, popular in Germany and readily available in UK supermarkets. It is very versatile and can be eaten hot or cold. It doesn't curdle when heated, and as such makes a great topping for this vegetarian moussaka.

SERVES 2

- 2 medium leeks, thinly sliced
- 2 medium courgettes, thickly sliced
- 1 fat clove garlic, crushed
- 250ml/9fl oz stock
- 2 tsp cornflour
- 1 tbsp chopped fresh dill or parsley
- 200g tub quark (skimmed-milk soft cheese)
- 1 free-range egg
- a little skimmed milk, optional
- 1 tbsp freshly grated Parmesan cheese
- sea salt and freshly ground black pepper

1 Simmer the leeks, courgettes and garlic in the stock in a shallow pan for about 3 minutes until just softened. Mix the cornflour with 1–2 tbsp water to a thin paste in a jug. Strain off the cooking liquid onto the cornflour paste, stirring briskly.

2 Tip the cooked vegetables into a shallow baking dish. Pour the cooking liquid back into the saucepan and heat again, stirring until thickened. Pour this over the vegetables and sprinkle over the chopped dill or parsley, plus seasoning to taste. The dish can be set aside to cool at this point if liked.

3 When ready to bake, heat the oven to 190°C/gas 5. Beat the quark with the egg and a splash or two of milk, if necessary, to make a soft cream. Spoon over the vegetables and sprinkle with the cheese. Bake for about 30 minutes until golden brown and lightly set. Cool for 10 minutes, then serve.

Slimmer's tip: You could omit the cheese and sprinkle with some Herby Wholemeal Topping Crumbs, page 158.

Leek and Pasta Salad with Crushed Pea Dressing

Crushing peas into a few spoons of Light Vinaigrette makes a delightful summery dressing, especially tossed into pasta and leeks. This recipe is a nice meal for one and combines leeks with cold wholewheat pasta – another food which (as you'll discover in the next chapter) has outstanding value for health protection – as well as fibre-rich peas. You could still be performing cartwheels at the age of 100 on dishes like this!

SERVES 1

- 50g/2oz dried wholewheat pasta shapes
- 2 medium leeks, trimmed and sliced
- 100g/3½oz peas
- 2 tbsp Light Vinaigrette, page 68, or fat-free vinaigrette
- 1 ripe tomato, chopped
- 2 tbsp chopped fresh mint
- sea salt and freshly ground black pepper

1 Boil the pasta according to pack instructions. Add the leeks 3 minutes before the end of the cooking time, then drain and rinse in cold water. Tip into a big bowl.

2 Cook the peas with 2 tbsp water either in a small pan or in the microwave for about 3 minutes. Then crush with a fork or masher into a rough purée. No need to drain. Mix in the vinaigrette and season to taste.

3 Toss into the pasta along with the tomato, and cool to room temperature. When ready to serve, mix in the mint and grind over more pepper to serve.

Leeks and Mushrooms à la Grecque

This could be a simple starter or a light lunch in the garden, served with a chunk of crusty bread to mop up the delicious juices. Use a small red onion if you don't have a shallot to hand.

SERVES 2

- 1 teaspoon coriander berries
- 1 shallot, thinly sliced
- 1 tbsp tomato purée
- 1 tbsp olive oil
- 1 tbsp red wine vinegar
- 1 clove garlic, crushed
- pinch cumin seeds
- 2 medium leeks, thinly sliced
- 125g/4oz baby-size button mushrooms, cleaned and trimmed
- 2 tbsp chopped fresh parsley
- sea salt and freshly ground black pepper

1 Crush the coriander berries in a pestle and mortar. (Or on a board with a rolling pin.) Place in a medium saucepan with 250ml/9fl oz water, the shallot, tomato purée, olive oil, vinegar, garlic and cumin seeds. Bring to the boil, then simmer for 2 minutes.

2 Drop in the leeks and mushrooms (halve the large ones, if necessary). Season to taste, bring to the boil, then simmer for about 5 minutes. Remove and cool. Stir in the parsley to serve.

Slimmer's tip: You could omit the oil to turn this into a virtually fat-free dish – too low in calories to make them even worth counting. To make it more substantial, but still ideal for slimming, you could add the butter beans from a small can.

Leek and Cauliflower Florentine

This is a healthy alternative to cauliflower cheese – without all that heart-threatening saturated-fat-packed cheese! Surprise yourself by discovering that it still makes a very tasty family-style supper despite being low-fat, low-cal and full of things that do you good. For a crunchy top, sprinkle with some Wholemeal Topping Crumbs and grill lightly until browned.

SERVES 2

- 2 medium leeks, sliced
- ½ small cauliflower, broken into small florets
- 150ml/5fl oz semi-skimmed milk
- 1 tbsp wholemeal flour
- 1 tsp stock powder or ½ stock cube, crumbled
- 1 tsp butter or low-fat spread
- good handful baby spinach leaves, chopped or shredded
- 1 free-range egg, hard-boiled and chopped
- about 3–4 tbsp dried Wholemeal Topping Crumbs, page 158, optional
- sea salt and freshly ground black pepper

1 Boil the leeks and cauliflower together in 250ml/9fl oz lightly salted water for 5 minutes. Drain, saving the water and returning it to the saucepan. Tip the vegetables into a shallow ovenproof dish.

2 Mix a little of the milk with the flour to a paste then mix in the remaining milk until smooth. Pour this into the pan with the vegetable water, along with the stock powder or cube, and the butter or low-fat spread. Bring slowly to the boil, stirring well until thickened and smooth, then mix in the spinach and cook for 1 more minute.

3 Remove from the heat, check the seasoning. Scatter the egg over the vegetables then pour over the sauce. If you want a nice crunchy top, sprinkle with the crumbs and brown under a preheated grill. Serve hot.

Leek and Prawn Stir-fry

This is a quick, healthy stir-fry for when you get home from work tired and hungry. Use large tiger prawns or the smaller cold-water prawns. The chilli adds a nice warming bite. Serve with some wholewheat spaghetti; much better for you than noodles.

SERVES 2

- 3 medium leeks, about 400g/14oz
- 1 large red chilli
- 1–2 fat cloves garlic, crushed
- 2 tbsp grated fresh ginger or ginger purée
- 2 tbsp vegetable oil
- 250g/9oz peeled cooked prawns, large or normal size, thawed if frozen
- 1 tbsp soy sauce
- 1 tbsp vermouth or dry sherry
- 1 tsp sesame oil
- 1–2 handfuls baby leaf spinach
- ½ tsp sesame seeds

1 Slice the leeks finely on the slant. Slit the chilli lengthways, shake out the seeds, then slice on the diagonal into rings. Mix together in a big bowl with the garlic, ginger and 1 tbsp oil.

2 Heat the remaining oil in a non-stick wok and when hot, toss in the prawns. Stir-fry for 1–2 minutes until they brown lightly, then tip out on to a plate. This initial frying gives them extra flavour.

3 Reheat the wok and toss in the leek mix. Stir-fry this for about 2 minutes until the leeks wilt. Return the prawns along with the soy sauce, vermouth or sherry, sesame oil and spinach, tossing until the spinach just wilts. Serve straight on two warm plates, sprinkled with the seeds.

Slimmer's tip: Tossing the vegetables first with oil helps them to get a good coating while using minimum oil. If you want to cut down on fat, omit the step of pre-frying the prawns and leave out the sesame oil. This turns the dish into an ideal one for dieters.

Shallots – add O-power the subtle way

Like all the onion family, shallots supply that very special ingredient that makes superbacteria thrive. Here the flavour is more subtle – oniony, yet not too pungent – making them a chef's favourite.

The lightly purple flesh is firmer too and less watery, which means when they cook down slowly, they turn a luscious caramel colour. The do-you-good recipes on the following pages are also a delight to eat.

Cook's notes

The downside of shallots is that they can be devils to peel, especially the smaller ones. Two ways round this are to soak the shallots in cold water for about half an hour to rehydrate the skins, or dunk them into a pan of boiling water for half a minute, then drain. The skins can then be slipped off more easily.

Chefs prefer to use the larger shallots, sometimes called banana shallots. One large banana shallot equals three smaller ones. And the smaller shallots can sometimes contain two bulbs, like twins. Where a recipe specifies shallots, assume these are the smaller ones, around 50–60g each. Baby-size shallots can be peeled and used whole.

Caponata – Sweet and Sour Ratatouille

This Sicilian vegetable dish contains the lovely fresh, summery, Mediterranean vegetables – peppers, aubergines and courgettes. Usually made with baby onions, we think it is wonderful with small shallots. Serve warm or lightly chilled with wholewheat pasta of your choice or a chunk of crusty wholemeal bread.

SERVES 4

- 12 shallots
- 1 small aubergine
- 1 medium courgette
- 1 red or yellow pepper, cored and quartered
- 2 fat cloves garlic, crushed
- 2 tbsp olive oil
- 300ml/½ pint tomato juice
- 2 tbsp balsamic vinegar
- juice ½ lemon
- 2 tsp sugar or 1½ tsp fructose
- 2 tbsp sliced black olives
- 2 tbsp capers
- 2 tbsp chopped fresh parsley
- sea salt and freshly ground black pepper

1 Dunk the shallots in boiling water for half a minute to soften the skins, then peel. Cut in half if large, so they are all roughly bite-size. Place in a big bowl.

2 Cut the aubergine, courgette and pepper into chunks. Add to the shallot bowl with the garlic and oil. Mix together well.

3 Heat a large non-stick frying pan or wok until hot, then toss in the oily vegetables and cook on a medium heat for about 5 minutes until just softened, shaking the pan once or twice.

4 Pour in the tomato juice, vinegar, lemon juice, sugar or fructose and seasoning. Continue cooking gently for about 10 minutes, then add the olives and capers and cook for another 5 minutes. Serve warm, not piping hot, sprinkled with parsley.

Slimmer's tip: If you want to cut out the oil to reduce the calories, simply put everything into a saucepan, from the shallots to the sugar, and simmer for 15 minutes, then finish the recipe as above.

Shallot and Potato Hotpot

A one-pot meal of everyday vegetables made delicious with healthy shallots. For a fuller meal, add some canned chickpeas, another rich source of good-bacteria-feeding fibre.

SERVES 2

- 4–6 shallots
- ½ green pepper, seeded
- 1 stick celery
- 1 fat clove garlic, crushed
- 1 tbsp olive oil
- 400g can chopped tomatoes
- 1–2 tsp chopped fresh oregano or ½ tsp dried
- 4 small–medium salad potatoes
- 125g/4oz cooked or canned chickpeas, optional
- 1 tbsp red wine vinegar
- sea salt and freshly ground black pepper

1 Peel the shallots and trim the root ends closely without removing them. This helps keep the bulb leaves together. Cut in half. Cut the pepper and celery into chunks, then mix them with the shallots, garlic and oil in a bowl until lightly and evenly coated.

2 Transfer to a saucepan and heat on medium until the vegetables start to sizzle. Cook for about 5 minutes until lightly golden, shaking the pan once or twice. Then tip in the tomatoes and about 100ml (3½fl oz) water plus the herbs and seasoning. Bring to the boil, then simmer for 10 minutes.

3 Meanwhile, scrub the potatoes and slice them thickly. Add to the pot and return to a simmer for 10–15 minutes until the potatoes are tender. Add the chickpeas, if liked, then mix in the vinegar and check the seasoning.

Slimmer's tip: To omit the oil, simply cook the vegetables, except the potatoes, and the herbs in the tomatoes with the water for 15 minutes, then add the potatoes and continue. This makes a very filling meal at low-calorie cost.

Seafood and Shallot Salad

Shallot vinegar has long been a classic accompaniment to fresh oysters, and makes a wonderfully light and tasty oil-free dressing for other seafood. It is now easy to buy packs of ready prepared seafood – prawns, squid rings and mussels – either fresh or frozen. So, if you enjoy a seafood lunch, then try this quick and simple meal. It also makes a great starter. If you prefer to lessen the pungency of the raw shallots, blanch them first in just-boiled water for about 10 minutes.

SERVES 2
- 3–4 shallots, chopped or thinly sliced
- 2 tbsp rice wine vinegar or red wine vinegar
- 1 small carrot, peeled
- 250g pack seafood cocktail medley, thawed if frozen
- 2 tbsp chopped fresh parsley
- 2 tbsp chopped fresh mint, optional
- 1 head chicory or baby gem lettuce
- sea salt and freshly ground black pepper

1 Mix the shallots (raw or blanched, see above) with the vinegar and some seasoning. Set aside to cool (if blanched).

2 Make very thin julienne (matchstick) strips of carrot. If you have a swivel vegetable peeler, then shave off several thin strips. Stack these on top of each other, 3–4 at a time, and cut into matchsticks.

3 Mix together the shallots, carrots, seafood, parsley and mint (if using). Separate out the chicory or lettuce leaves and line two shallow bowls. Pile the seafood in the centre and serve.

Slimmer's tip: Rice wine vinegar is a lighter, slightly sweet alternative to wine or cider vinegars, sometimes sold as 'sushi dressing'. It makes an excellent oil-free salad dressing and is increasingly sold in supermarkets in the Oriental foods section.

THE OLIGO-AWKWARD SQUAD

Asparagus
Jerusalem Artichokes
Chicory

WE DID SAY THAT bifidobacteria were pretty picky eaters, and their other three food favourites come with inbuilt snags: asparagus, which shouts out for loads of buttery saturated fat; Jerusalem artichokes – knobbly root veg which pose how-to-peel-and-deal-with-them problems, and chicory – a 'wonder what to do with that' sort of veg, which has a stronger and more distinctive flavour than most.

These problem-solver recipes provide the answers and turn these super health-foods into tasty treats.

Asparagus without butter

Say Bye-bye to the butter and Hello to the lovely flavour of asparagus served the healthy way with these recipes. Each provides a very low-cal, low-fat solution to what to eat for lunch when you are trying to shed weight.

Asparagus can be cooked either by light steaming or char-grilling on a ridged griddle pan. For steaming, there is no need to buy an expensive tall asparagus pan; cheap collapsible metal baskets that fit inside most saucepans are perfect. Or if you already have a ridged metal griddle pan for cooking meat and fish, use this for asparagus spears too.

Asparagus and Poached Egg

You might like to serve the poached egg on a slice of wholemeal toast with the asparagus alongside.

SERVES 1

- 100g/3½oz asparagus spears
- a couple of dashes soy sauce
- 1 tbsp wine vinegar
- 1 large organic free-range egg, ideally very fresh
- sea salt and freshly ground black pepper

1 Trim the spears and cut in half if long. Either place in a steamer basket, sprinkle with soy sauce and steam for 2–3 minutes until al dente, then remove with a slotted spoon onto a warm plate, or, to char-grill, heat the pan until a strong heat is rising, then place the spears directly on the base and cook for 2–3 minutes each side until lightly scored.

2 Meanwhile, put a medium pan half full of water on to boil and add the vinegar and ½ tsp salt. Break the egg into a cup.

3 Using a long wooden-spoon handle, stir the water briskly so it forms a vortex and gently tip the egg in. The swirling water will help set the egg into a neat shape.

4 Poach gently for about 2 minutes until the white is firm and the yolk still soft. Remove with a slotted spoon and dab with a paper towel to remove excess water. Slide the egg on top of the asparagus spears and grind over some pepper.

Miso Soup with Asparagus

Miso is fermented soyabean paste (sometimes with added barley or rice), high in minerals and flavour. Sachets of miso soup are sold four to a pack as instant packet soups and found in an increasing number of supermarkets. You simply tip a sachet into a mug and mix in boiling water. Then add a choice of chopped fresh vegetables and maybe some cubes of tofu. Asparagus tips or snipped fine stems of asparagus can be stirred straight into the hot liquid without any cooking. A great, speedy, healthy lunch for one. Perfect at the office.

SERVES 1
- 1 sachet instant miso soup mix
- about 4 thin asparagus spears, ends trimmed
- 2 baby corns, optional
- 1 spring onion, chopped
- few small cubes tofu, optional
- few dashes of soy sauce

1 Dissolve the contents of the sachet in a mug of boiling water.

2 Slice the asparagus thinly on the diagonal, and do the same with the corn, if using.

3 Mix into the soup along with the onion and soy sauce to taste. Add a few small cubes of tofu, if liked, and serve immediately. The heat of the soup is just enough to take the raw edge off the vegetables.

Asparagus and Corn with Onion Salsa

The Argentinians have a popular chopped onion salsa called chimchurri. It is served with a variety of dishes, and teams up perfectly with warm asparagus. Use milder red onions or the sweet white Viladia onions.

SERVES 2

- 250g/9oz thick asparagus spears, trimmed
- 6 baby corns
- sea salt and freshly ground black pepper

SALSA

- 1 small red onion or ½ Viladia onion, finely chopped
- 1 large fresh green or red chilli, seeded and finely chopped
- 2 tbsp chopped fresh parsley
- 2 tbsp fresh lemon juice
- ½ tsp dried oregano
- 1 clove garlic, crushed

1 First make the salsa to let the flavours marinate. Put the chopped onion into a big bowl. Add the chilli, parsley, lemon, oregano, garlic and seasoning. Mix well and set aside for an hour or so.

2 When ready to serve, put a pan of salted water on to boil. Fit a metal steamer basket in the pan. Cut the spears in two and slice the corns on the diagonal. Steam both together, lightly seasoned, for 2–3 minutes until just tender.

3 Remove the vegetables to two warmed plates and spoon the salsa over. Serve warm, not too hot.

Cook's note: If you prefer to soften the flavour of raw onion, blanch the chopped flesh in a pan of boiling water for ½ minute, then drain. Rinse in cold water and shake well to drain.

Easy ways with Jerusalem artichokes

These often underrated and brilliant bioactive vegetables are in season during the mid-winter months. The skins may look daunting, knobbly and beige-grey in colour, but their humble appearance belies their superb flavour and bountiful health benefits. Farmer's markets are a good source of supply. And there is no need to peel these little beauties. If they are a bit earthy, soak them in tepid water to loosen any dirt, then scrub clean with a stiff brush. Shave off any tiny knobs and slice thickly or chop as required.

Jerusalem artichokes are not related to the thistle-like globe artichokes, although they do taste similar, so don't confuse the two. They have a delicious aromatic flavour and creamy texture, perfect for soups and savoury bakes, but you will find they also make great salads, either raw or blanched for a few minutes.

The name has nothing to do with Jerusalem, either – it is derived from the Italian word *girasole*, the sunflower, because as the plant grows in the field, it follows the sun round, as do sunflowers.

Artichoke and Shallot Salad

Artichokes make a great winter salad if blanched first to retain a light crunchy texture. In this dish they are mixed with other more colourful winter vegetables – shallots, carrots and fennel. This recipe is ideal for thinner artichokes, if you want to save the larger, rounder ones for soups and roasting.

SERVES 2

- ½ small bulb fennel
- 1 medium carrot
- 250g/9oz Jerusalem artichokes, well scrubbed
- 2–3 tbsp Light Vinaigrette, page 68
- 2 shallots, chopped
- 50g bag rocket leaves or baby leaf salad or watercress
- 2 tbsp chopped roasted hazelnuts, optional
- sea salt and freshly ground black pepper

1 Slice the fennel as thinly as possible, ideally using a mandolin or Japanese food slicer, then dunk in a bowl of ice-cold water for 15 minutes so it crisps up. Drain well and pat dry with a tea towel.

2 Peel the carrot and slice into long thin ribbons using a swivel vegetable peeler.

3 Trim off any little knobbles on the artichokes, then slice into rounds the thickness of a £1 coin. Blanch in a pan of salted boiling water for 2 minutes, then drain and set aside in a bowl. Toss with 1 tbsp vinaigrette, season well and mix with the fennel and carrot ribbons.

4 When ready to serve, mix with the rocket, salad leaves or watercress and remaining vinaigrette. Divide between two plates and sprinkle over the nuts, if liked. Serve lukewarm.

Cook's note: For a big main-meal salad, you could halve and grill a small goat's cheese crottin and serve on top of each plate.

Artichoke and Mushroom Soup

Many top chefs rate artichoke soup as one of the great winter dishes. The vegetables may look humble but their fragrance is a perfect base for a memorable meal. Here we cook them with another popular winter vegetable, mushrooms. For a sophisticated soup, use a handful of wild mushrooms along with the ordinary ones. Nice served with Low-fat Oven Croûtons, page 159.

SERVES 4

- 500g/1lb 2oz large Jerusalem artichokes, well scrubbed and finely chopped
- 1 medium onion, chopped
- 2 cloves garlic, crushed
- 2 tbsp olive or sunflower oil
- leaves from 1 large sprig fresh thyme
- 500ml/18fl oz vegetable or chicken stock, made with a cube
- 500ml/18fl oz skimmed milk
- 100g/3½oz mushrooms, trimmed and sliced
- squeeze fresh lemon juice
- 2 tbsp chopped fresh parsley
- sea salt and freshly ground black pepper

1 Put the artichokes, onion and garlic into a large saucepan and stir well with the oil, 3 tbsp water and thyme leaves. Heat until sizzling, then cover, reduce the heat to low and cook gently for about 10 minutes, shaking the pan once or twice. Try not to lift the lid until 10 minutes is up or you let out the steam.

2 Pour in the stock and season to taste. Bring to the boil and simmer, uncovered, for another 10 minutes until the artichokes are softened. If you want a creamy texture, press the artichokes with a masher or crush against the side of the pan with a fork. Alternatively, blitz in a blender until very creamy and return to the pan.

3 Pour in the milk and mushrooms and return to a simmer for another 5 minutes. Check the seasoning and add the lemon juice but do not allow to boil. Serve sprinkled with the parsley.

Slimmer's tip: Omit the oil for a low-fat version of this soup. Simply cook the chopped artichokes gently in half the stock for 10 minutes then proceed with the rest of the recipe. Freeze any leftovers in portions.

Balsamic Roasted Artichokes

Oven-roasting chunks of Jerusalem artichokes with other sweet winter vegetables is so simple to do and a wonderfully chic way to eat healthily. A plateful of these is particularly filling, especially topped with a few shavings of Parmesan cheese, some crisp green cabbage and a chunk of crusty wholemeal bread. The tangy roasting juices make the sauce.

SERVES 2

- 250g/9oz Jerusalem artichokes, scrubbed
- 1 large carrot
- 2 shallots or one medium red onion
- 1 red or yellow pepper, cored
- leaves from 1 sprig fresh thyme or rosemary
- 1 tbsp olive oil
- 1 tbsp balsamic vinegar
- 2–3 tbsp chopped fresh parsley
- sea salt and freshly ground black pepper

1 Heat the oven to 190°C/gas 5. Cut the artichokes and carrot into even bite-size chunks. Halve the shallots or cut the red onion into thick wedges. Cut the pepper into eighths.

2 Tip the vegetables into a large food bag then add the herbs, oil and vinegar. Seal the bag and shake it very well, rubbing the vegetables together so they are all evenly coated.

3 Tip out onto a shallow roasting pan and season. Roast for 15 minutes, shaking the pan once. Then pour in a large cup of water and return the pan to the oven for another 5 minutes. The vegetables should be just softened, lightly browned and totally delicious. Serve in shallow bowls sprinkled with the parsley.

Cook's note: For a more substantial main meal, top with about 20g/¾oz fresh Parmesan shavings or dot some low-fat soft cheese on top and scatter over 1 tbsp pinenuts.

Chefs' ways with chicory

What we British call chicory, the French call 'endive' and the Dutch 'witloof'. But whatever the name, the health properties are universal, and the flavour and compact crisp heads make them ideal for hot or cold dishes.

Cook's note

Chefs like to braise chicory slowly in the oven covered with a thin layer of stock. Chicory heads can also be slit in two and grilled or pan-fried with a smear of oil, cut-side down until they caramelize lightly. As a snack you can peel off the leaves one at a time to dip into dressing, or perhaps the Beany Butter on page 75, or fill with some cold leftover ratatouille as a starter. The other big plus for chicory is that it keeps a good few days in the fridge without wilting. During the winter months you can buy red-coloured chicory heads (called *radicchio di Treviso*), which look marvellous on their own or mixed with the lime-green variety. When preparing chicory, core the heads first – using the tip of a small, sharp knife, remove the core at the base of each chicory head in a cone shape.

Orange Braised Chicory

Surprisingly for a salad vegetable, chicory needs long slow cooking to develop its delicious sweet flavour. This makes a nice light lunch dish with juices you could mop up with crusty bread.

SERVES 2

- 4 even-sized large heads chicory
- 2 tsp icing sugar
- 1 tbsp olive oil
- 300ml/½ pint light stock (vegetable or chicken)
- juice 1 small orange
- 1 tbsp chopped fresh parsley
- sea salt and freshly ground black pepper

1 Preheat the oven to 180°C/gas 4. Core the chicory (see facing page), then split each head lengthways. Lay them cut-side up on a board and dust over the icing sugar from a little sieve. This helps them caramelize nicely.

2 Heat a large non-stick pan gently and add the oil, then place the chicory sugar-side down in the pan and cook for a minute or so until lightly browned. Remove to a shallow ovenproof dish.

3 Heat the stock and add the orange juice. Pour over the chicory, season to taste, cover and bake for 45–50 minutes, uncovering for the last 10 minutes to reduce some of the cooking liquid. Cool for 10 minutes, then serve, sprinkled with parsley.

Cook's note: Instead of orange juice, you could use a small glass of tomato juice.

Balsamic Char-grilled Chicory with Raisins and Pinenuts

Chicory grills well on a hot griddle pan or BBQ. This dish is nice served alongside grilled sardines, mackerel, salmon or tuna. Or try it with a little grilled goat's cheese crottin each.

SERVES 2
- 4 heads chicory, red or green
- 3 tbsp raisins
- 2–3 tbsp balsamic vinegar
- 2 tbsp pinenuts, lightly toasted
- sea salt and freshly ground black pepper

1 Preheat a barbecue grill or non-stick griddle pan. Core the chicory (see page 46) and split in half. Soak the raisins in a little boiling water to cover for 5 minutes, then drain. This plumps them up.

2 Place the chicory heads cut-side down on the hot grill or griddle and cook (ungreased) for about 5 minutes, checking that they do not burn but develop attractive char-grilled stripes. Flip over and cook the other side briefly, until just wilted.

3 Remove to a platter, season and cover with cling film for 15–20 minutes. The steam rises and helps soften the leaves a little more and moisten them.

4 When ready to serve, drizzle over the balsamic and scatter with the raisins and nuts.

Chicken and Chicory Salad

Use two skinned and cooked chicken breasts combined with leaves of crisp bitter-sweet chicory for a light but filling salad. The dressing is creamy but low in fat.

SERVES 2
- 2 heads chicory
- 1 small red onion, thinly sliced
- 6–8 cherry tomatoes
- 2 skinless, boneless cooked organic chicken breasts
- small handful rocket leaves
- sea salt and freshly ground black pepper

DRESSING
- 1 tbsp Light Vinaigrette, page 68, or fat-free dressing
- 2 tbsp half-fat crème fraiche or low-fat natural yogurt
- 1–2 tsp Dijon or French mustard
- 1 tsp clear honey

1 Core the chicory (see page 46) and separate out the leaves. As you get nearer the centre, you may have to cut away the leaves. Set aside. Soak the red onion in a big bowl of cold water for 15 minutes, then drain and pat dry.

2 Halve the tomatoes. Slice the chicken on the diagonal or cut into bite-size chunks.

3 Whisk together the dressing ingredients, adding some cold water to thin it down, if liked.

4 Arrange the chicory leaves attractively on two plates. If you like, tear them into pieces. Scatter over the onion, tomatoes, chicken and rocket leaves, and season. Drizzle with the dressing and serve.

Cook's note: For an alternative dressing, use fresh lemon juice instead of the vinaigrette.

2

Dishes you *shouldn't* resist

DIETARY FIBRE, the undigested part of plants, is a complex substance made up of a number of components. These vary to some degree in different plants. In some plants, the fibre includes a substance called resistant starch, which has recently been revealed to have outstanding benefits in strengthening the immune system.

New studies not only outdate the old concept that all starchy food is bad for you, but show that the starch in certain foods has a more powerful beneficial impact on good bacteria than anything else you might eat.

It is now known that an average of 10 per cent of the starch we eat passes undigested through the body (a useful weight-control bonus there!) to feed those good bacteria in the colon. And, when they feed on this resistant starch, good bacteria become hyper-active in delivering just what the doctor ordered – large quantities of a substance called butyrate.

Butyrate is particularly strongly linked with protection from cancer. It not only keeps the cells in the gut wall healthy, it has also been shown to inhibit the growth and proliferation of tumour cells.

A number of foods provide us with some resistant starch. Beans (see next section) are among them, and there is a little in bread, cornflakes and rice. But the outstanding sources in our diet are rather an odd collection. They are – wait for it:

Bananas...

... when eaten with their skins slightly green. When fully ripe their resistant starch turns to sugar.

Pasta and potatoes...

... when cooked then eaten cold in salads. Strange though this may sound, when these foods are cooled, some of their starch is converted back (retrograded) into a form resistant to digestion. More of it passes through to the colon to feed good bacteria.

Make your menus richer in resistant starch by regularly introducing recipes from this section.

Bring on those bananas

The obvious way to eat greenish bananas for their health impact is to simply slice one into your breakfast cereal each morning. That's fine. But they also make ideal ingredients for fruit smoothies and fruit salads.

'Greenish'? Well, we aren't asking you to force them down ultra-firm and flavourless. As long as the stalk end of the banana is green and the yellow skin slightly tinged with green, the fruit inside remains high in that precious resistant starch. But you know how fast they ripen, so buy only two or three at a time. And go for organic if possible.

Winter Fruit Salad

There is something very comforting and convenient about a fruit salad made with dried fruits. Even better, they are packed full of fibre and, being naturally sweet, need no added sugar. Use the no-need-to-soak fruits for speed. Instead of syrup, make a mugful of aromatic Earl Grey tea or use one of your favourite fruit teas.

SERVES 4

- 250ml/9fl oz hot tea, such as Earl Grey or your favourite fruit tea
- 1 cinnamon stick or ½ tsp ground cinnamon
- 1–2 strips orange peel, optional
- 6 dried apricots, halved
- 6 stoned prunes
- 75g/3oz dried mango or peach or papaya, snipped
- ½ x 75g pack dried cranberries
- 2 greenish bananas, thickly sliced
- 1 dessert apple, cored and sliced

1 Pour the hot tea into a medium bowl and add the cinnamon stick, or ground cinnamon, and the strips of orange peel, if liked.

2 Then mix in the dried fruits, from apricots to cranberries. Leave to steep until tepid, then remove the cinnamon and peel strips.

3 Mix in the banana and apple slices and chill until required.

Cook's note: If you prefer to add a little sweetness to this, drizzle in 2 tsp clear honey or 1 tsp fructose powder.

Tropical Rum Fruit Salad

Chopped almonds add a lovely crunchy surprise to fruit salads, and sliced dates and rum-soaked sultanas are among our other favourite ingredients. They go particularly well with sliced greenish bananas. Pineapple pieces and a fresh just-ripe mango continue the tropical theme.

SERVES 4

- 2 tbsp sultanas
- 2 tbsp rum
- 227g can pineapple pieces in natural juice
- 1 small mango or 1 kiwi
- 2 large greenish bananas
- 3 semi-dried dates, such as Medjool, stoned and sliced
- 2 tbsp roughly chopped blanched almonds

1 Put the sultanas and rum in a small saucepan and heat gently until just bubbling, then remove. Alternatively, place in a small heatproof bowl and microwave for 30 seconds – to just heat the rum. Remove and cool for 15 minutes while you finish the salad.

2 Tip the pineapple into a medium bowl with the juice. Peel the mango, then cut off the flesh in small bite-size chunks. Or if using kiwi, peel and cut into chunks. Add to the pineapple.

3 Slice the banana thickly on the diagonal and stir in, along with the dates and almonds.

4 Allow to marinate for at least 30 minutes, although you could cover and chill this for a good day before serving.

Banana and Summer Fruits Smoothie

Smoothies are really liquid fruit salads – so popular now that they are sold, quite expensively, ready-made. Make your own at home more cheaply and drink it really fresh and frothy. You will need a good liquidizer or blender for this; a food processor can't crush ice cubes so well. Alternatively, omit the ice cubes and drink it like a milk shake. Greenish bananas make the best bases for smoothies and blend well with almost all other fruits.

SERVES 1–2

- 3 ice cubes
- 1 small glass cold skimmed milk, about 150ml/¼ pint
- 1 medium-size greenish banana
- 3 medium ripe strawberries, hulled
- a handful (about 3 tbsp) blueberries
- a handful (about 3 tbsp) raspberries
- 1 tsp clear honey, optional

1 Put the ice and milk into a blender or liquidizer and break in the banana. Whiz on a slow speed until the ice cubes become crushed, then increase the speed for a few seconds.

2 Drop in the other fruits and honey, if using, then whiz again until frothy and thick. Pour into 1 large or 2 smaller glasses and serve immediately. A good smoothie is too thick to sip through a straw.

Cook's notes: For a more exotic tropical flavour, use chopped ripe mango and/or papaya. A ripe kiwi fruit is nice, as are ripe peaches, squashy plums and apricots. A few chunks of ripe pineapple are good, and the pulp of passion fruit makes a heavenly smoothie. But the base should always be some ice cubes, milk and an almost ripe banana.

Full-on pasta power

Wholewheat pasta has a particularly high content of total dietary fibre. Cool it to make a pasta salad and it also becomes a rich source of that invaluable resistant starch. Here are three versions of one of the healthiest, most health-protective lunches you can eat.

Cook's notes

Wholewheat pasta has a delicious nutty bite to it. You can buy it in shapes or as spaghetti. The texture of wholewheat pasta is very slightly chewy but it cooks to an attractive creamy colour and takes only around 10 minutes or so. Wholewheat spaghetti makes a good higher-fibre substitute for Chinese or Japanese noodles, although it helps if you break the sticks in half before cooking. One healthy tasty cook's tip is to dress pasta for salads with vinaigrette dressing just after cooking. As the pasta cools it absorbs flavour and so needs less dressing later to taste delicious. The same principle holds true for potato salads too.

Tuna, White Bean and Pasta Salad

This is an ideal after-work supper dish when time is short but you want a healthy and filling meal. The onion is lightly blanched in the same pan as the pasta, which lessens the impact of raw onion on the breath.

SERVES 2

- 125g/4oz wholewheat pasta shapes
- 1 small red onion, thinly sliced
- 2 tbsp Light Vinaigrette, page 68
- 200g can tuna chunks in brine or spring water
- 410g can cannellini beans, drained
- 1 tomato, chopped
- 1 tbsp capers
- 3–4 leaves fresh basil torn or 1 tbsp chopped fresh parsley
- sea salt and freshly ground black pepper

1 Boil the pasta in plenty of lightly salted water according to pack instructions. Add the red onion slices 1–2 minutes before the end of cooking so they soften a bit. Drain both and rinse in some cold running water, then mix with the dressing.

2 Drain and coarsely flake the tuna. Rinse the beans in cold water and shake well. Mix both into the pasta with the tomato, capers and herbs. Set aside to cool and chill lightly. Check the seasoning and serve.

Slimmer's tip: For a low-fat version, omit the vinaigrette and use 1 tbsp fresh lemon juice or rice wine vinegar and 1 tbsp low-fat natural yogurt.

Spanish Chickpea and Pasta Salad

Here we mix wholewheat pasta with chickpeas, sweet peppers and paprika for an aromatic Spanish-style dish. This salad, combining so many outstandingly healthy foods, is the essence of famous-for-fitness Mediterranean eating. It would be extra nice served with a handful of baby leaf spinach, torn lettuce or a few blanched whole green beans.

SERVES 2

- 125g/4oz wholewheat pasta shapes
- 1 red or yellow pepper, cored and thinly sliced
- 1 red onion, thinly sliced
- 1 tbsp olive oil
- 1 tsp paprika
- 1 tsp oregano
- 410g can chickpeas
- 2 tbsp chopped parsley or coriander
- sea salt and freshly ground black pepper

1 Boil the pasta in salted boiling water according to pack instructions. When al dente (just tender), drain and rinse in cold water.

2 Meanwhile, put the pepper and onion slices into a saucepan with the oil and 2–3 tbsp water. Heat until sizzling, then cover and cook gently for about 5 minutes.

3 Uncover and mix in the paprika and oregano. Cook for 1 minute more then toss in the pasta and chickpeas. Season well and cook for another 2–3 minutes.

4 Mix in the chopped herbs just before serving.

Slimmer's tip: For a fat-free variation, omit the oil and cook the pepper and onion gently in a little water until softened, or use some of the chickpea-can liquor.

Japanese 'Noodle' and Vegetable Salad

Fibre-rich wholewheat spaghetti has a texture similar to Japanese buckwheat or soba noodles. This is a great salad to take as a lunchbox meal – ideal for slimmers.

SERVES 2
- 125g/4oz wholewheat spaghetti, broken in half
- 100g pack asparagus tips
- 2–3 spring onions, chopped
- 3 baby corns, thinly sliced
- 3–4 radishes, sliced
- 1 carrot, coarsely grated
- 125g/4oz marinated firm tofu (e.g. Cauldron), cut in small cubes, optional
- 1 tbsp chopped fresh coriander or parsley

DRESSING
- 1 clove garlic, crushed
- 1 tbsp soy sauce
- 2 tsp mild chilli sauce, optional
- 1 tsp sesame oil
- 1 tbsp finely chopped peanuts
- ½ tsp ground cumin
- ½ tsp ground coriander
- 1 tbsp rice wine vinegar
- 1 tsp clear honey

1 Make the dressing – put all the dressing ingredients into a small saucepan with 100ml/3½fl oz water. Bring to the boil, stirring, then set aside.

2 Boil the spaghetti according to pack instructions. Add the asparagus tips for the last 2 minutes. Drain and rinse in cold water for a few seconds, shake dry and tip into a bowl.

3 Mix in the hot dressing and allow to cool. Then add the remaining vegetables, herbs, and tofu, if liked. Check the seasoning and serve.

Potato-plus salads

Potatoes, like pasta, become one of the richest sources of hugely valuable resistant starch when eaten cold. Forget that long discredited low-carb nonsense. Potatoes, unless cooked in fat or served with great globs of fatty mayonnaise, aren't particularly high in calories and are, in fact, a healthy food. Super healthy when you eat them cold.

In these recipes we've specified 'light' mayonnaise and kept the quantity moderate. We've also mixed in vegetables such as peas, asparagus and spring onions to add extra flavour and even greater bio-benefits, turning a little of what you fancy into a healthy cocktail.

Cook's notes
Choose potatoes that are slightly waxy in texture, such as Charlotte, Nicola, Maris Piper, Pink Fir Apple and, of course, the ultimate new potato – Jersey Royals. No need to peel them, just scrub and boil whole or cut into equal-sized pieces. After boiling, season well and toss with a little Light Vinaigrette dressing (page 68), then leave to cool. This helps boost the flavour without making the salad taste greasy. The best potato salads are always made with freshly boiled potatoes, not cold leftover ones you find lurking in the fridge. Potato salads will keep for up to three days if chilled, so why not make a double batch? And a final little tip is to check salads for seasoning just before serving, as cold food often needs a little more help in the flavour department.

Quick and Easy Potato Salad

This basic potato salad can have additional extras according to your taste. Just add one or two of those suggested below. A few sliced red radishes would add some lovely colour as a garnish, and the salad can be served on a few frilly lettuce leaves or set off with those superbacteria-friendly chicory leaves.

SERVES 2

- 300g/10oz new potatoes, scrubbed
- a big sprig fresh mint, optional
- 2 tbsp Light Vinaigrette, page 68
- 2–3 spring onions, lightly trimmed and chopped
- 5cm/2in piece cucumber, chopped
- 2 tbsp Creamy Mock Mayo, page 69
- 3 red radishes, sliced, to garnish
- sea salt and freshly ground black pepper

ADDITIONS, CHOOSE ONE OR TWO

- 100g/3½oz asparagus tips or thin asparagus spears, chopped
- 100g/3½oz frozen peas, blanched and cooled
- 1 medium leek, thinly sliced and blanched
- 1 head chicory, coarsely shredded

1 Cut the potatoes into small bite-size chunks and boil in salted water with the mint until just tender, 10–12 minutes. Drain, rinse briefly in cold running water, then shake well. Tip into a bowl, remove the mint sprig, season and toss in the vinaigrette dressing. Leave to cool.

2 When cold, mix in the onions, cucumber and mayo. Then add additional ingredients, above, according to choice. Check the seasoning, garnish with the radishes and serve lightly chilled.

Slimmer's tip: To reduce the fat, omit the mayo and use 2 tbsp low-fat natural yogurt.

Potato and Spicy Bean Salad

For a powerfully healthy potato salad, mix in some fibre-rich canned pulses as well. A potent partnership to 'energize' your good bacteria! A can of mixed pulses is easy, and ideal because of the colour and texture of the beans. This salad would make a perfect lunchbox meal and a double quantity could be served at a small barbecue.

SERVES 2

- 300g/10oz small new potatoes
- 3 tbsp Light Vinaigrette, page 68
- ½–1 tsp mild chilli powder or paprika or mild curry powder
- 1 shallot, or large spring or salad onion, thinly sliced
- 410g can mixed pulses or red kidney or pinto beans, drained
- ½ small red pepper, cored and finely chopped
- 1–2 tbsp chopped fresh parsley or chives
- 100g bag watercress sprigs or rocket, to serve, optional
- sea salt and freshly ground black pepper

1 Cut the potatoes into bite-size chunks and boil until tender, about 10–12 minutes. Drain, rinse in some cold running water and shake dry. Tip into a bowl and toss with 2 tbsp vinaigrette and the spice, and season well.

2 Meanwhile, if liked, soak the sliced shallot or onion in cold water for about 15 minutes to lessen the raw flavour, then drain and pat dry. Mix with the potato, then leave until completely cool.

3 Add the pulses, pepper, herbs and remaining dressing, then chill until required. Check the seasoning, and serve in shallow bowls surrounded by the cress or rocket.

New Potato and Apple Salad

The Germans have a great range of potato salads, not all smothered in high-fat mayo dressings. The secret of a good flavour is to dress the potatoes with vinaigrette just after cooking. Apples and mustard are favourite co-ingredients, and pickled onions add a tangy touch. This salad is perfect to serve with grilled oily fish, such as mackerel or tuna, or with hard-boiled eggs.

SERVES 2
- 6 baby-size new potatoes, about 300g/10oz weight, halved
- 2 tbsp Light Vinaigrette, page 68
- 1 tsp coarse grain mustard
- ½ Granny Smith apple
- 1 tbsp reduced-fat crème fraîche
- 12 small pickled onions, preferably silverskin onions in sweet vinegar, or pickled Borettane onions, halved
- 2 tbsp chopped dill or parsley
- sea salt and freshly ground black pepper

1 Boil the potatoes in lightly salted water until just tender, about 10–12 minutes.

2 Drain and tip into a bowl and mix with the vinaigrette, seasoning and mustard. Cool to room temperature.

3 Core and chop the apple into small chunks, then mix into the potatoes with the crème fraîche and onions.

4 Leave until quite cold, then stir in the chopped herbs. If chilled ahead, then allow to stand for 20 minutes or so before serving.

Slimmer's tip: For a low-fat dressing, use 2 tbsp rice wine vinegar instead of the vinaigrette and low-fat natural yogurt instead of crème fraîche.

Light salad dressings

It's the dressing, as well as the choice of vegetables, that makes the difference between a super-healthy salad and one that can pile on the pounds. Don't assume that everything sold as salad is good for you. Those mayonnaise-rich carton-packed and fast-food restaurant salads can be positively counterproductive when it comes to keeping a healthy weight. So go easy on the quantity of dressings you use and opt for lighter versions using these recipes.

Light Vinaigrette

This vinaigrette uses twice the quantity of oil to vinegar rather than the usual three-to-one proportions. This does produce a slightly sharper flavour so add a little honey (or apple juice if you prefer) to counter the acid. The dressing keeps well in the fridge so it's worth making a big batch.

MAKES ABOUT 250ML/9FL OZ – A MEDIUM JAM JAR

- 6 tbsp olive oil
- 6 tbsp sunflower or vegetable oil
- 6 tbsp rice wine or white wine vinegar
- 1 clove garlic, crushed, or 2 tsp garlic purée, optional
- 2 tsp Dijon mustard
- 1 tsp clear honey
- ½ tsp fine sea salt
- ¼ tsp freshly ground black pepper

1 Put all the ingredients into a large jam jar and shake vigorously to blend.

2 Store in the fridge and shake well again whenever required.

Slimmer's tip: Reduce the calories in the dressing with the addition of 100ml/3½fl oz water to the mix.

Creamy Mock Mayonnaise

Make up a small jar of this and store it in the fridge; use 2–3 tablespoons per dish. It will keep for up to a week. Perfect for potato salads.

MAKES ABOUT 150ML/5FL OZ

- 3 tbsp olive, sunflower or vegetable oil
- 3 tbsp white wine vinegar
- 1 tsp Dijon mustard
- ½ tsp fine sea salt
- a few grindings fresh black pepper
- 4 tbsp reduced-fat crème fraîche or fat-free fromage frais

1 Simply whisk everything in a bowl and scoop into a small jam jar.

FLAVOUR VARIATIONS – CHOOSE ONE

Add 1 tbsp fresh lemon juice
Add 1–2 tbsp chopped fresh chives or parsley
Add ½ to 1 tsp mild curry powder
Add 1–2 tsp coarse grain mustard instead of Dijon
Add 2 tsp crumbly blue cheese, e.g. Stilton. Mash with some of the dressing then blend in.

Slimmer's tip: A squeeze or two of fresh lemon or lime juice plus some crushed sea salt and freshly ground black pepper makes a virtually calorie-free dressing. Also, rice wine vinegar, sometimes sold as sushi dressing, makes a delightful dressing, light and slightly sweet. Just sprinkle on as much as you like – it is also calorie-free.

3

The great all-rounders – beans!

BECAUSE OF THEIR multiple health benefits, beans (all those varieties sold dried or canned, rather than those eaten in the pod) have bounced right to the top of the league of healthy foods during the past decade. The latest US government dietary guidelines urge Americans to eat beans and other pulses several times a week. The same advice is coming loud and clear from all leading health authorities. If you were to look for one food as the top superfood, beans must be a major contender for the title.

Beans, as long as they are eaten together with grain-based foods as they usually are (e.g. beans on toast or bean soup with bread), are just as valuable a source of protein as any animal product. The protein they supply comes without the heart-threatening fat of many dairy products, or the colon-threatening risk of red and processed meats. It is now known that it is exceedingly hard to go short of protein, even if you follow a vegetarian or vegan diet. The hazards of eating too much of it in the form of meat and dairy products far outweigh the unlikely risk of going short of it.

Long known as a rich source of dietary fibre, beans are now known to contain fibre of a particularly valuable kind. Resistant starch and oligosaccharides are both present in significant quantities. So it isn't surprising they have been found to have so many beneficial impacts on health.

Beans

- Protect you against disease by their particularly beneficial bio-action.
- Lower bad cholesterol (as effectively as oats) to protect your heart.
- Help to keep blood-sugar levels on an even keel to protect against diabetes.
- Supply particularly valuable nutrients, such as iron and B vitamins.

It's great that beans can be open-a-can easy (no need to use dried beans unless you prefer to) and the basis of so many delicious meals. The varied recipes on the following pages show what a versatile part they can play in everyday eating.

Cook's notes

Beans are sold dried or conveniently ready-cooked in cans, with or without added salt and sugar. The canned liquor can be used if liked, otherwise rinse the beans under cold running water and shake dry. Canned beans are excellent for use in home cooking, additive and preservative free, and just as valuable nutritionally as the dried kind – so use them with confidence.

Cooked or canned beans can be puréed to add a creamy texture to soups or pasta sauces in place of high-fat cream. It's a neat cheat. For portion sizes, a 410g can will feed 2 people, with a drained weight of about 220–230g per can.

If you prefer to use dried beans, they will need pre-soaking, with timing depending on the variety. Place them in a big bowl and cover with cold water to a depth of at least 7–8cm/3in above the beans. Ideally, allow at least 6–8 hours, but you can shorten this to 2–3 hours by covering them with boiling water before draining and cooking. However, this may cause the skins to wrinkle and split.

To cook, cover with more cold water at least 5cm/2in above the beans and add a sliced onion and bay leaves or rosemary sprigs to the water. Boil for a good 10 minutes to destroy any potential mild toxins that might cause a dull tummy ache, then lower the heat to a simmer. Beans can be cooked in a third of normal time in a pressure cooker (check instruction book for full details), or in a microwave using a deep non-metallic bowl and covering the top with cling film that has been slightly vented to allow steam to escape. Cooked dried beans freeze very well, so you may like to soak and cook extra quantities for another time. Beans expand to between two and two and a half times their dried weight. Allow about 50g/2oz dried beans a head.

Beany Butter

Whenever you feel a snack-attack coming on, and a little 'something on toast' is in order, try this lower-fat substitute for very high-fat peanut butter: a creamy spread of butter beans. It's quite delicious, we assure you. Make a batch and store in the fridge. It will keep for up to a week and will be enough for a slice of toast every day.

MAKES ABOUT 250G/9OZ FOR 5–6 SLICES TOAST
- 410g can butter beans
- 2 tbsp extra virgin olive oil
- 1 small clove garlic, optional
- ½ tsp ground cumin
- 1 tsp sea salt
- freshly ground black pepper

1 Drain the beans and place in a food processor along with the olive oil, garlic, cumin and seasoning.

2 Whiz until smooth and creamy, then spoon into a medium-size jam jar and chill. Spread on slices of hot wholemeal toast.

Slimmer's tip: Halve the oil if you want to cut right down on fatty calories, but a little is necessary for flavour.

Succotash – American Bean and Vegetable Soup

Americans are very fond of lima beans, which are smaller versions of our butter beans. This chunky vegetable soup is said to be based on a Native American dish and combines butter beans and sweetcorn. For a creamy texture without high-fat cream, purée or crush half the beans. This soup freezes well.

SERVES 4

- 2–3 sticks green celery, lightly trimmed and thinly sliced
- 1 large onion, chopped
- 1 green pepper, cored and chopped
- 2 tbsp olive or sunflower oil
- 1.5 litres/2½ pints vegetable or chicken stock (can be made with a cube)
- 2 x 410g cans butter beans, drained
- 1 x 200g can sweetcorn, drained
- 2 tbsp chopped fresh parsley or coriander
- 1–2 tbsp fresh lemon juice
- sea salt and freshly ground black pepper

1 Put the celery, onion and pepper into a large saucepan with the oil and 4 tbsp water. Heat until sizzling, then cover, turn the heat down and cook gently for about 7 minutes. Add the stock with seasoning to taste and bring to the boil. Simmer for 10 minutes.

2 Meanwhile, purée 1 can of beans in a food processor or crush with a fork or potato masher. Stir into the pot with the other can of beans and the sweetcorn, then return to a simmer for 5 minutes. Serve with the chopped herbs stirred through and add lemon juice to taste just before serving.

Slimmer's tip: For a very low-fat version, omit the oil and increase the water in step 1 to about one third of a mug.

Cream of Bean Soup with Paprika Drizzle

Use any of your favourite beans for this recipe – butter beans are our preference. To give this creamy yet low-fat soup extra eye appeal, drizzle with a little runny paprika paste.

SERVES 4
- 1 onion, chopped
- 1 clove garlic, chopped
- 1 tbsp olive oil
- leaves from 1 sprig fresh thyme
- 1 tsp chopped fresh or ½ tsp dried rosemary
- 2 x 410g cans butter beans
- 500ml/18fl oz vegetable or chicken stock
- 500ml/18fl oz skimmed milk
- 1 tsp ground paprika
- sea salt and freshly ground black pepper

1 Mix the onion, garlic, oil and herbs in a saucepan and stir to coat then add 2 tbsp water. Heat until sizzling, then cover and cook in a low heat for about 10 minutes until softened.

2 Add the beans with can liquor and stock. Season, bring to the boil, cover, then simmer for 10 minutes. Strain most of the liquid into a jug. Whiz the pan contents in a food processor or blender for a good 2–3 minutes until very smooth. Gradually add back the saved liquid and return to the pan.

3 Stir in the milk and return to a simmer for 2–3 minutes. Check the seasoning. Mix the paprika with 1 tsp cold water. Pour the soup into warmed bowls and drizzle with the paprika paste, swirling with a teaspoon. Serve immediately.

Brown Basmati Bean Burgers

A cross between the texture of a fish cake and a bean burger, these highly nutritious little patties even look like traditional burgers when cooked. The recipe makes eight, so allow two each; any left over can be frozen and used for single meals later.

SERVES 4

- 100g/3½oz brown basmati rice
- 2 tbsp sunflower oil
- 1 onion, finely chopped
- 1 small green pepper, cored and chopped
- 2 cloves garlic, crushed
- 1 tsp ground paprika or mild chilli
- 1 tsp ground cumin
- 1 tsp ground coriander
- 1 tsp dried oregano
- 410g can red kidney beans, drained
- 50g/2oz mature Cheddar cheese, grated
- 3–4 tbsp wholemeal flour, for coating
- sea salt and freshly ground black pepper

1 Cook the rice in plenty of lightly salted water to cover, allowing to slightly overcook until quite soft, about 30–35 minutes. Drain, season and cool.

2 In large saucepan, mix 1 tbsp oil with the onion, pepper and garlic until coated, then heat until it begins to sizzle. Add 2 tbsp water, cover and sweat the vegetables for about 10 minutes. Mix in the spices and oregano and cook for 1 minute. Mix in the rice.

3 Put the beans into a food processor and pulse until they form a crushed but still chunky purée, or crush finely with a fork. Mix this into the pan along with the cheese – you should have a firm mixture. Check the seasoning, then spoon the mixture onto a dinner plate and spread to an even layer. Cool, then chill until cold. (*continued on p. 80*)

4 Divide the mixture into 8 equal sections and press each into a neat round patty, coating your hands in the flour if the mixture sticks. Toss the patties in more of the flour to coat evenly, shaking off excess. Lay on a sheet of non-stick baking parchment.

5 Heat a non-stick frying pan and trickle in half the remaining oil. Swirl it around the pan. Lay in four of the burgers and cook on a medium heat for 2–3 minutes each side until browned and crisp. Turn carefully with a fish slice so they don't crack. Repeat with the remaining oil and burgers. Good with Squashy Balsamic Tomatoes, page 173.

Slimmer's tip: You could omit the Cheddar cheese, or use 25g/1oz of grated medium-fat fresh Parmesan cheese instead. To cut down on oil during frying, use a low-fat spray.

Cook's note: Leftover burgers can be frozen in a single layer on a cake tray, then bagged up when solid. When you want a couple of burgers, thaw 20–30 minutes and reheat in a medium-hot oven for 10–12 minutes.

Tortilla Wraps with Crushed Red Beans and Avocado

Wraps (soft corn tortillas) are very popular now as an alternative to sandwiches. Unfortunately, there aren't any wholemeal tortillas sold in the UK, but the fibre in the beans will compensate. This is a quick and easy recipe. If you want a spicy bean filling, use a can of chilli beans.

SERVES 2

- 410g can red kidney beans or red kidney beans in chilli sauce
- 2 spring onions, chopped
- 2 soft corn tortillas
- 4 tsp extra-light Philadelphia soft cheese (5 per cent fat)
- 1 tomato, chopped
- 1 small ripe avocado, peeled and thinly sliced
- sea salt and freshly ground black pepper

1 Drain the beans, including the chilli beans if using. The spicy flavour will still be present. Lightly purée in a food processor, using the 'pulse' button, to a chunky texture, then mix in the onions.

2 Warm the tortillas by wrapping in foil and placing in a low oven for 5–10 minutes. Then spread them first with the cream cheese and then with the bean mixture.

3 Season lightly, then sprinkle with the chopped tomato. Halve, stone and scoop out the flesh of the avocado, then slice thinly and divide between the tortillas. Roll them up, cut each in half and serve. Best eaten with fingers, so don't forget a napkin.

Slimmer's tip: Use 2 tbsp quark (zero-fat soft cheese) instead of the cream cheese and substitute shredded lettuce or a handful of baby spinach leaves for the avocado. Avocado oil is healthy oil but, as far as weight is concerned, avocados are a rich source of unwanted calories.

Smoked Haddock and Bean Cassoulet

Traditionally a cassoulet is a rich bean and meat stew with high-fat sausages, duck and goose fat. But a low-fat cassoulet can be just as tasty and full of healthy F2 foods. This dish can be made the day before you need it, so the flavours develop.

SERVES 2

- 350g/12oz chunky smoked haddock fillet
- 1 tbsp olive oil
- 1 onion, chopped
- 1 small stick celery, chopped
- 1 small carrot, chopped
- 1 fat clove garlic, crushed
- 2–3 tbsp dry white wine, optional
- 410g can cannellini beans, drained
- 200g can chopped tomatoes
- 200ml/7fl oz fish or vegetable stock
- leaves from 1 sprig fresh thyme
- 1 tsp chopped fresh rosemary or ½ tsp dried
- pinch saffron strands, optional
- 2 tbsp Wholemeal Topping Crumbs, page 158
- 2 tbsp chopped fresh parsley
- sea salt and freshly ground black pepper

1 Skin the fish by running a sharp knife between the flesh and skin (or ask the fishmonger to do this for you). Check the flesh for bones and pull any out with your fingertips or tweezers. Cut the fish into bite-size pieces. Set aside.

2 Stir the oil with the onion, celery, carrot and garlic in a saucepan and add 2 tbsp water. Heat until sizzling, then cover and cook gently for 5 minutes until softened. Add the wine, if using, and cook for 1 minute, then mix in the beans, tomatoes, stock and herbs. Bring to the boil.

3 Meanwhile, mix the saffron with 1 tbsp hot water to dissolve, then add to the pot. Turn the sauce down to a simmer and cook for 10 minutes.

4 Drop in the cubes of fish and cook for another 2–3 minutes. They don't need long. Season to taste.

5 Heat the oven to 190°C/gas 5. Tip the cassoulet into a shallow ovenproof dish and sprinkle with the crumbs and parsley. Bake for 10–12 minutes until the top becomes crunchy. Cool for 10 minutes before serving.

Slimmer's tip: This is already an ideal dish for dieters, but if you want to cut out all fatty calories, omit the oil entirely and simply sweat the vegetables first in a little extra stock.

Black Bean Gumbo

Gumbo is a popular Creole dish, named after the African-American name for the vegetable okra. Black beans are among the few beans not sold in cans, so first you need to soak and boil them. Serve with plain brown basmati rice.

SERVES 4

- 150g/5oz dried black beans
- 1 large sprig fresh thyme
- 2 tbsp olive oil
- 1 onion, sliced
- 2 fat cloves garlic, crushed
- 1 small green pepper, cored and diced
- 250g/9oz fresh okra
- 1 tsp ground cumin
- 1 tsp mild chilli powder
- 400g can chopped tomatoes
- 150ml/¼ pint vegetable stock
- 1 tbsp chopped fresh basil or coriander
- sea salt and freshly ground black pepper

1 Soak the beans in plenty of cold water for at least 24 hours.

2 On the day of serving, drain the beans and place in a large saucepan covered with more cold water to a depth of at least 5cm/2in. Add the thyme. Bring to the boil and cook for 10 minutes, then lower the heat and simmer gently for 1–1½ hours until the beans are tender. They will not become very soft but keep an eye on the water level, topping up with boiling water from a kettle if it evaporates. When cooked, drain, rinse in cold water and tip into a bowl. Season and mix in 1 tbsp oil. Leave to cool.

3 Put the onion, garlic, pepper and remaining oil into the same saucepan. Add 2–3 tbsp water, heat until sizzling, then cover and sweat for about 10 minutes until softened.

4 Meanwhile, trim the okra stalks and cut in half. They will ooze a little sticky sap, which is fine, but it is best to cut them just before cooking. Pop the okra into the pan along with the spices, tomatoes, stock and seasoning. Bring to the boil, then simmer for 10 minutes.

5 Add the beans and continue cooking for another 5 minutes, then serve, sprinkled with herbs. Nice with rice – brown basmati is best.

Slimmer's tip: If you want to omit the oil, don't use any to dress the hot beans in step 2, halving the quantity in the recipe.

Brazilian Bean-stuffed Peppers

Bean-stuffed peppers are popular family food in many parts of South America and eaten almost every day. This is a typical main-course dish, colourful and full of flavour. It is easier to make a four-portion quantity and freeze half, if necessary, for another meal. If so, thaw the frozen peppers when needed, then reheat in the oven at 190°C/gas 5 for about 15 minutes until piping hot.

SERVES 4

- 4 peppers, green, red or yellow
- 1 onion, chopped
- 2 fat cloves garlic, crushed
- 1 tbsp olive oil
- 1 tsp ground coriander
- 400g can chopped tomatoes
- 1 tbsp fresh chopped basil or oregano
- 420g can red kidney or pinto or borlotti beans, drained
- 100g/3½oz goat's cheese, crumbled or grated
- 2 tbsp Wholemeal Topping Crumbs, page 158
- sea salt and freshly ground black pepper

1 Halve the peppers lengthways and scoop out the seeds; trim the stalk but don't remove. Blanch the pepper shells in boiling water for 3 minutes, then drain upside down.

2 Mix the onion and garlic with the oil in a saucepan and heat until sizzling. Mix in 2–3 tbsp water and the coriander, then cover and cook gently for 10 minutes until softened.

3 Add the tomatoes, herbs and beans. Season well and cook for another 10 minutes, then take off the heat and mix in half the cheese. Lay the pepper shells in a shallow ovenproof dish and fill with the bean mixture. Sprinkle with the remaining cheese, then the crumbs.

4 Brown the peppers under a preheated grill until hot and bubbling. If you intend freezing half the peppers, then don't grill them at this stage, but later when they have thawed and been reheated.

Slimmer's tip: You could omit the oil and sweat the onion and garlic in a little water instead. To make a very low-cal dish you could also leave out the cheese and simply sprinkle peppers with the crumbs.

Borlotti Bean and Spinach Cannelloni

This is a dish for all the family to enjoy, or you could divide it into two 2-portion servings, freezing one of them in a foil container for another meal for two. Use lasagne sheets to form the cannelloni rolls – much easier than trying to stuff filling down tubes.

SERVES 4

- 1 onion, chopped
- 2 fat cloves garlic, crushed
- 1 tbsp olive oil
- 500g carton chopped tomatoes with herbs or 400g can
- 410g can borlotti beans, drained
- 8 green lasagne sheets (200g/7oz)
- 125g/4oz baby leaf spinach
- 100g/3½oz half-fat mozzarella, sliced into 8
- ½ x 200g carton reduced-fat crème fraîche
- 25g/1oz finely grated fresh Parmesan
- 2–3 tbsp Wholemeal Topping Crumbs, page 158
- sea salt and freshly ground black pepper

1 Mix together the onion, garlic and oil in a saucepan and add 2 tbsp water. Heat until sizzling, then cover and cook gently for 10 minutes until softened. Add the tomatoes and cook for another 5 minutes.

2 Meanwhile, crush the beans roughly with a fork or put in a food processor and pulse lightly to crush. The beans should be still a little whole. Mix this into the sauce and season to taste. The mixture should be quite thick but not dry. Cool.

3 Blanch the pasta sheets, 4 at a time in a large pan of boiling water for 2 minutes. Using a slotted spoon, lift them out into a big bowl of cold water, then drain and pat dry.

4 Heat a non-stick frying pan or wok until hot and dry fry the spinach until it just wilts. Remove to a colander and press down with a wooden spoon to squeeze out any moisture.

5 Lay out the pasta sheets on a board. Spoon the bean mixture at one end (about 2 tbsp a time), then divide the spinach and mozzarella among the sheets, placing on top of the bean mixture. Roll up, pushing back in any filling that spills out. Lay in a shallow ovenproof dish, join side down. If you have any bean filling left over, spoon this on top.

6 Dollop with the crème fraîche and sprinkle with the Parmesan and crumbs. Heat the oven to 190°C/gas 5. Bake for 15–20 minutes until hot and bubbling. Cool for 10 minutes before serving.

Slimmer's tip: Instead of crème fraiche use half a 200g carton of quark, thinned until just smooth and runny with about 3 tbsp skimmed milk.

Two Bean, Root Vegetable and Quark Pasta

This is a great autumn or winter one-pot meal. The sauce is a light tomato one with some quark drizzled over. As an unusual topping, try the dry-fry crunchy spaghetti.

SERVES 2

- about 50g/2oz wholewheat spaghetti, optional
- 100g/3½oz wholewheat pasta shapes
- 125g/4oz whole green beans, trimmed and halved
- 1 red onion, sliced
- 1 medium-small turnip, trimmed and chopped
- 1 small carrot, trimmed and chopped
- 1 small parsnip, trimmed and chopped
- 1 tbsp olive or sunflower oil
- ½ tsp dried mixed herbs, such as Herbes de Provence

- 400g can chopped tomatoes
- 250ml/9fl oz vegetable stock
- 410g can mixed pulses or any beans of choice
- 3 tbsp quark
- sea salt and freshly ground black pepper

1 If you want to make the crunchy topping, heat a non-stick frying pan and when it feels hot, crush in the spaghetti in short lengths. Cook, stirring, until they start to brown and become crisp, then tip out onto a side plate and cool. Set aside.

2 Boil the pasta shapes according to pack instructions, adding the green beans for the last 2–3 minutes. Drain, rinse under cold water and season lightly. Set aside also.

3 Put the onion and chopped vegetables into a saucepan and mix in the oil. Heat until it starts to sizzle, then add 3 tbsp water and the herbs, cover and cook gently for 10 minutes until softened, stirring once or twice.

4 Stir in the tomatoes, stock and pulses, season and bring to the boil, then simmer gently for 5 minutes or so. Mix in the pasta and green beans and check the seasoning.

5 Beat the quark with a little cold water to thin it down to the consistency of pouring cream. Dish the pasta between two shallow bowls, then drizzle over the runny quark, sprinkle with the crunchy spaghetti and serve.

4

The rise of the lowly lentil

THE ONCE LOWLY lentil has worked its way up the fashion food chain. Chic chefs now love to serve lentils, particularly green and Puy varieties, with fish or chicken. It's a food in tune with today's focus on healthy eating, one of the richest of all sources of fibre. Lentil fibre includes those particularly valuable oligosaccharides and some resistant starch, but lacks the cholesterol-lowering value of the fibre in beans. On the bonus side it is less likely to produce those – ahem – antisocial consequences. And it simply isn't true that you always have to soak lentils for hours.

Cook's notes

There are lentils a-plenty in supermarkets, delis and Asian food shops, from the versatile red split lentils to the rustic green (aka 'continental') lentil and the gourmet Puy lentil that even has its own French *appellation contrôlée*. But other lentils to search out are Canadian *lentilles verts*, the chic Italian Castelluccio and the Indian masoor lentils (which are in fact un-split red lentils). Some packs tell you to soak lentils first, but we find all of them can be tipped straight from the pack into the pot and cook in 10 to 20 minutes, depending on the variety.

Red split lentils make quick soups and sauces and 2–3 tbsp can be used as a thickening agent, like flour, adding extra fibre to boot. Just sprinkle into a simmering stew, pasta sauce or soup for the last 10–15 minutes of cooking.

Winter Vegetable and Lentil Soup

Possibly the most classic of lentil soups – perfect for healthy comfort eating.

SERVES 4
- 1 onion, chopped
- 1 medium turnip, trimmed and finely chopped
- 2 leeks, thinly sliced
- 1 medium carrot, chopped
- 150g/5oz red split lentils
- 1.5 litres/2½ pints stock

- leaves from 1 sprig fresh thyme or a good pinch dried
- 1 bay leaf
- 1 tsp chopped fresh rosemary or a good pinch dried
- quarter small Savoy cabbage, cored and shredded
- sea salt and freshly ground black pepper

1. Put the onion, turnip, leek, carrot, lentils, stock and herbs into a large saucepan. Bring to the boil, season, then lower the heat to a simmer.

2. Cook for about 15–20 minutes until thickened and the vegetables are soft. Remove the bay leaf.

3. Meanwhile, blanch the cabbage shreds in boiling water to cover for a minute or so, then drain in a colander and immediately rinse under cold water. This fixes the bright green colour.

4. Tip the cabbage into the soup pot and reheat gently. Check the seasoning and serve.

Slimmer's tip: This virtually fat-free soup makes a very low-calorie lunch for those aiming to speed off a few pounds or kilos.

Cook's notes: Those without weight worries could first gently fry 2–3 finely chopped rashers of organic streaky bacon in the pan. Then add the first 4 vegetables and sweat them gently for 5 minutes before adding the remaining ingredients and cooking from the rest of step 1. Lentils and bacon are a popular combination but bacon – one of those 'processed meats' linked by research with colon cancer – should only be eaten in modest quantities like this.

Italian Mushroom and Lentil Soup

The dainty golden-brown Italian Castelluccio lentils have a delicious lightly nutty flavour that is wonderful cooked into soups, especially with mushrooms. Use either fresh chestnut mushrooms or, for a treat, a pack of dried wild porcini mushrooms (ceps). If you can't find Castelluccio lentils, use green (continental) lentils instead.

- 1 onion, chopped
- 1 small stick celery, chopped
- 1 small carrot, chopped
- 1 tbsp olive oil
- 2 tbsp dry vermouth or sherry, optional

- 150g/5oz chestnut mushrooms, finely chopped, or 20g pack porcini mushrooms
- 150g/5oz Castelluccio or green lentils
- 1.5 litres/2½ pints stock
- sea salt and freshly ground black pepper

1 Mix the onion, celery and carrot in a saucepan with the oil and 2 tbsp water, then heat until sizzling. Cover and sweat for about 5 minutes, then add the vermouth or sherry and cook for another minute.

2 Meanwhile, if using the dried mushrooms, soak them in just enough boiling water to cover for about 5 minutes until softened. Strain the liquid into a cup, chop the flesh and add both to the pan. If using fresh mushrooms stir them into the pan along with the lentils, stock and seasoning.

3 Bring to the boil, then lower the heat to a gentle simmer and cook for about 20 minutes until the lentils are very soft. Check the seasoning and serve.

Warm and Spicy Lentil Soup

The inspiration for this soup comes from North Africa, where lentils are often used in delicious, aromatic soups. Whizzed to make a silky creamy textured soup and sprinkled with fresh herbs, this one is quite good enough for a dinner party.

SERVES 4

- 180g/6oz red split lentils
- 1 carrot, chopped
- ½ small green pepper, cored and chopped
- 1 tbsp grated fresh root ginger or ginger purée
- 2 fat cloves garlic, crushed
- 1.5 litres/2½ pints stock
- 1–2 tsp ground cumin
- ½ tsp ground turmeric
- juice ½ lemon
- 1 tbsp chopped fresh chives
- some small sprigs fresh coriander
- sea salt and freshly ground black pepper

1 Put all the ingredients from the lentils to the spices into a large saucepan and add some seasoning to taste.

2 Bring to the boil, stirring once or twice, then lower the heat to a gentle simmer and cook for 15–20 minutes until the lentils have burst open and the vegetables are soft.

3 Add lemon juice to taste and check the seasoning. Serve garnished with the herbs.

Lentil-stuffed Marrow

Marrows are really just large courgettes, yet they seem to suffer a bad press and be regarded as boring. Not so with this tasty lentil and tomato stuffing drizzled with a light pesto dressing. Perfect for a warm early autumn supper when marrows are at their best. Use green lentils for this dish.

SERVES 2

- 1 medium-size marrow, about 1kg/2¼ lb
- 125g/4oz green (continental) lentils
- 4 tomatoes
- 1 onion, chopped
- 1 fat clove garlic, crushed
- 1 small red or yellow pepper, cored and chopped
- 1 tbsp olive oil
- 2 tbsp pinenuts, optional
- 1 tbsp pesto
- 2–3 tbsp dried wholemeal breadcrumbs, page 158
- 2 sprigs fresh basil
- sea salt and freshly ground black pepper

1 Slit the marrow lengthways in two. Using a pointed teaspoon, scoop out the seeds. Then remove the flesh, taking care not to nick the skin, and chop into small chunks. Set aside.

2 Boil the lentils according to pack instructions, making sure they are not too soft and retain a little texture. Drain and season lightly.

3 Dip the tomatoes into a pot of boiling water for a few seconds, then peel off the skins. Chop roughly, discarding the cores. Heat the oven to 190°C/gas 5. Blanch the marrow shells in a large pan of boiling water for a minute or so until just softened, then drain upside down.

4 Stir the onion, garlic and pepper in a saucepan with the oil, add 2 tbsp water and heat until sizzling, then cover and cook on a low heat for 5 minutes until softened.

5 Uncover and add the chopped marrow and tomatoes, plus seasoning to taste, then continue cooking on a gentle heat for a further 10 minutes until tender. Taste for seasoning and add the lentils and, if using, the nuts.

6 Put the two marrow shells into a baking dish snug enough to hold them both upright, then fill them with the lentil mixture. Blend the pesto with 2 tbsp water. Trickle over both marrows and sprinkle with the crumbs. Bake for 20–25 minutes until crisp on top. Garnish with the basil sprigs.

Kastoori – Lentils with Rice and Pasta

This is a popular daily dish from the Middle East, which, like many dishes from that region, is full of F2 goodies. It is certainly good comfort food, filling, wholesome and fat-free. Use green (continental) or Puy lentils. Serve either with Squashy Balsamic Tomatoes (page 173) or make a quick homemade fat-free tomato sauce to dollop on top.

SERVES 2

- 100g/3½oz brown basmati rice
- 100g/3½oz green or Puy lentils
- 60g/2oz wholewheat pasta shapes
- 1 onion, chopped
- 1 fat clove garlic, crushed
- 1 large green chilli, seeded and chopped, optional
- 1 tsp ground cumin or mild curry powder
- 1 tsp sea salt
- freshly ground black pepper

SAUCE

- ½ onion, roughly chopped
- 400g can chopped tomatoes with herbs or spices
- a few dashes mild chilli sauce or Worcestershire sauce
- 1–2 tbsp chopped fresh coriander or parsley

1 Soak the rice and lentils in a large bowl of cold water for 5 minutes, then drain and place in a large saucepan. Add the pasta, onion, garlic, chilli (if using), spice, salt and pepper and 750ml/1¼ pints water.

2 Bring to the boil, stirring, then cover and lower the heat. Cook, without lifting the lid, for 25 minutes. Remove from the heat and allow to stand for 5 minutes, then uncover and fork gently through.

3 Meanwhile, for the sauce, simply put the ingredients into a non-stick saucepan, bring to the boil, season to taste, then simmer for 5–10 minutes until slightly reduced. Mix in the herbs and serve with the kastoori.

Cook's note: If you have no weight worries you could pre-fry the onions, garlic, chilli and cumin in 1 tbsp oil for extra flavour before adding the rice, lentils and pasta.

Lentil Soufflé Bake with Wholemeal Toasts

Try this recipe when you want an impressive healthy family main meal. And please don't feel you can't make a soufflé. It's just a matter of timing and being able to whisk egg whites stiffly. Red lentil purée makes a healthy alternative to thick white sauce, which is used in most soufflés. Serve with a nice green salad.

SERVES 4

- 3 slices wholemeal bread
- a little low-fat spread, optional
- 180g/6oz red split lentils
- 1 onion, finely chopped
- 1 carrot, finely grated
- 600ml/1 pint stock or water
- ¼ tsp dried mixed herbs
- 40g/1½oz freshly grated Parmesan
- 2 free-range organic eggs, separated
- sea salt and freshly ground black pepper

1 Make fresh breadcrumbs with 1 slice of bread using a food processor or blender. Cut the crust from the other 2 slices and spread very thinly with the low-fat spread, if using. Cut into triangles and press these round the sides of a small flan dish, about 20cm/8in across. Set aside.

2 Put the lentils, onion, carrot, stock or water and herbs into a large saucepan with about ½ tsp salt and pepper to taste. Bring to the boil, then cover and simmer gently for about 20 minutes. Uncover and bubble for a minute or so longer if the mixture is quite wet. It should be soft but not mushy.

3 Beat in the breadcrumbs and the cheese, cool for 5 minutes, then mix in the egg yolks.

4 Preheat the oven to 180°C/gas 4. Whisk the egg whites until stiff but not dry. Beat 1 tbsp whites into the lentil mix then gently fold the rest in with a large metal spoon.

5 Scoop this into the bread-lined dish, smoothing the top. Bake for about 25–30 minutes until risen and golden, then serve immediately.

Lentil Lovers' Bolognese

Red split lentils can make a great pasta sauce in around 15 minutes, just as long as it takes to cook the pasta. You can enjoy this sauce as it is, or jazz it up further with a chopped courgette and red pepper. Serve with wholewheat spaghetti or pasta shapes, sprinkled with a little freshly grated Parmesan cheese or dried Wholemeal Topping Crumbs. The recipe serves four, so you could freeze what you don't eat.

SERVES 4

- 1 onion, chopped
- 2 fat cloves garlic, chopped
- 1 tbsp extra virgin olive oil
- 3–4 tbsp dry white wine, optional
- 125g/4oz red split lentils
- 1 tsp dried oregano
- 400g can chopped tomatoes

- 1 tbsp tomato purée
- 1–2 tbsp chopped fresh parsley, to serve, or dried Wholemeal Topping Crumbs, page 158
- sea salt and freshly ground black pepper

1 Put the onion and garlic into a saucepan and stir in the oil until well coated. Add 2 tbsp water and heat until sizzling. Turn the heat to medium and cook for about 5 minutes until softened. Add the wine, if using, and cook for a minute or so until evaporated.

2 Stir in the lentils, oregano, chopped tomatoes, tomato purée and about 250ml/9fl oz water. Season well, bring to the boil, then simmer for 10–12 minutes. By this time the sauce should have thickened. You can boil the pasta at the same time and either serve it tossed into the sauce or with the sauce spooned on top. Sprinkle with parsley or crumbs.

Cook's notes: You can spike the basic recipe above with a crumbled dried red chilli, 3–4 chopped anchovies (patted dry of oil), 2 tbsp chopped olives and 1 tbsp capers to make a Puttanesca sauce. Or add a can of tuna in brine, drained and flaked.

Lentil Pilaff with Cod or Salmon

Top chefs love to serve grilled fish accompanied by a delicious lentil dish. This lentil mix also goes nicely with grilled chicken or roasted root vegetables, such as sweet potato and peppers. Use Puy, green or Castelluccio lentils.

SERVES 2

- 125g/4oz small lentils, such as Puy, green or Castelluccio
- 1 onion, chopped
- 1 small carrot or turnip, coarsely grated
- ½ small bulb fennel or 1 stick celery, chopped
- 400ml/14fl oz stock
- 1 bay leaf
- 1 sprig fresh thyme
- 2 tbsp chopped fresh parsley
- 1 tbsp Light Vinaigrette, page 68
- 2 cod or salmon fillets, skin on, about 100g/3½oz each
- fresh lemon wedges, to serve
- sea salt and freshly ground black pepper

1 Put the lentils, onion, carrot or turnip, fennel or celery, stock, bay leaf and thyme into a large saucepan with ½ tsp salt and pepper to taste.

2 Bring to the boil, then cover and simmer very gently for about 20 minutes. The mixture is best very slightly wet. Check the seasoning and mix in the parsley and vinaigrette. Set aside.

3 Heat a grill or non-stick griddle pan. If using a grill, place a sheet of foil on the rack just large enough for the fish. Cook the fish skin-side up for 3–4 minutes until crisp, then using a spatula turn it carefully and cook for a further 2 minutes. Season after cooking, and serve the fish on a bed of the lentils with the lemon wedges alongside.

Chicken and Lentil Curry

Ready-made and take-away curries are often very high in fat, so it's better to make your own at home. This quick and easy recipe uses chicken breasts. Always choose organic chicken, which not only tastes better but contains less fat than the usual factory-farmed birds. (Factory-farmed birds are now much fattier than pre-war chickens.) Like many Indian-style dishes, this one uses lots of onion as well as red split lentils to thicken the sauce. Very F2! Serve with plain boiled brown basmati rice mixed with peas, fresh or from frozen.

SERVES 2

- 1 onion
- 1 fat clove garlic
- small knob fresh root ginger, about 2cm/¾in, roughly chopped
- 2 tsp mild curry powder
- 2 skinless, boneless organic chicken breasts, about 100g/3½oz each
- 1 tbsp tomato purée
- 100g/3½oz red split lentils
- 1–2 tbsp fresh lemon or lime juice
- 2 tbsp chopped fresh coriander
- 1 tbsp lightly toasted flaked almonds, optional
- sea salt
- freshly ground black pepper

1 First, make a spice purée. Whiz together the onion, garlic, ginger and curry powder in a blender or food processor until smooth. Scoop out into a non-stick saucepan and cook on a gentle heat for about 2 minutes, stirring once or twice.

2 Cut the chicken into bite-size pieces and pop into the pan. Cook for 1–2 minutes until just firm, then mix in the tomato purée, lentils, 300ml/½ pint water and seasoning. Bring to the boil, stirring, then lower the heat right down, cover and cook for 10–12 minutes until the sauce thickens and the chicken is cooked.

3 Stir in the lemon or lime juice and coriander and check the seasoning. Serve topped with the almonds and yogurt, if liked, and accompany with boiled basmati rice into which you have mixed about 100g/3½oz cooked peas.

Cook's note: You could turn this into a fish curry by adding cubes of raw cod or salmon. In this case, make the sauce as in step 2 and omit the chicken. Add the fish halfway through the 10–12-minute cooking time. Vegetarians could substitute about 150g/5oz whole baby mushrooms and stir in 100g/3½oz baby leaf spinach for the last 5 minutes of cooking. Alternatively, use a 250g pack of minced or chunks of Quorn in step 2.

Lemony Lentil and Carrot Salad

Try this salad in the summer when you want a light salad that is more than just a few leaves with tomato. It is also far healthier than the salads smothered in high-fat mayo-style dressings. Use Puy, green or Castelluccio lentils.

SERVES 2

- 125g/4oz small lentils, such as Puy, green or Castelluccio
- 2 tbsp Light Vinaigrette (page 68)
- ½ tsp ground cumin
- 2 tbsp fresh lemon juice
- 2 spring onions, chopped
- 1 carrot, coarsely grated
- 1 small head chicory
- 2 tbsp chopped fresh mint
- frilly lettuce, such as oak leaf
- sea salt and freshly ground black pepper

1 Cover the lentils in cold water to a depth of about 2cm/¾in and bring to the boil. Cook according to pack instructions until just tender but still holding their shape then drain, rinse under cold water and shake dry.

2 Tip into a big bowl, season nicely then mix with the vinaigrette, cumin, 1 tbsp lemon juice, the onions and carrot. Leave to cool.

3 Separate out the outside chicory leaves until you reach the tightly packed core. Slice the core into thin rings and mix into the lentils together with the mint and remaining lemon juice.

4 Arrange the lettuce and chicory leaves on 2 plates, spoon the lentils on the centre and serve.

Cook's note: To make this more of a main-meal salad, top with quartered hard-boiled eggs or grilled chicken or tuna steaks.

5

Pea power!

WHETHER CHICKPEAS OR green peas – fresh, frozen, dried, mushy, sugarsnap or mangetout – all types of peas have health-protective power as rich sources of good bacteria-feeding fibre. The following recipes can ease them deliciously into your diet.

Cook's notes

Peas include the versatile chickpea (popular in many cuisines from India to the Mediterranean and on to Mexico), dried yellow and green peas – which can be husked and described as split – and, of course, fresh peas in many forms, including those sold still nestled in their pods like mangetouts (French for eat-all). Chickpeas hold their shape and texture well, even if overcooked. Canned chickpeas are excellent. The Spanish call them garbanzos and revere them as one of the great classic foods, while in the Middle East and Greece they are soaked and puréed raw to make classic hummus.

Split yellow and green peas are perfect for soups because they dissolve during long slow cooking into a creamy purée. They can be cooked straight from the pack but benefit from soaking overnight for a lighter texture. Much is made of the vitamin content of fresh 'garden' peas but, usually, frozen peas have higher levels because they are blanched and frozen within a couple of hours of picking. A bag of frozen peas is one of the healthiest foods you can enjoy, and they also taste sweeter and less mealy than fresh. Stir-fry or steam podded peas such as sugarsnaps, because they only need the lightest of cooking.

Chickpea and Roasted Pepper Pâté

A flavourful alternative to the usual fatty pâtés. Serve it with hot triangles of wholemeal toast, or with leaves of chicory and sticks of carrot.

SERVES 4

- 1 red pepper, cored and quartered
- 410g can chickpeas
- 1 fat clove garlic, roughly chopped
- 2 spring onions, roughly chopped
- ½–1 tsp mild chilli powder
- ½–1 tsp ground cumin
- 100g/3½oz extra light Philadelphia soft cheese (5 per cent fat)
- sea salt and freshly ground black pepper

1 Heat a grill until hot, then place the pepper quarters skin-side up in the rack. Grill until the skin starts to blacken and blister. Remove the grill tray and cover the peppers with a clean cloth. Leave for 5 minutes, then peel the skin. Chop the flesh and set aside.

2 Drain most of the liquid from the chickpeas, leaving about 3 tbsp. Place in a food processor with the garlic, spring onions, chilli powder and cumin to taste, plus some seasoning. Whiz to a chunky purée.

3 Then spoon in the soft cheese and pulse until just mixed. You want to leave the pâté with some texture.

4 Scoop from the processor bowl and mix in the chopped peppers, check the seasoning and spoon into 4 ramekin dishes. Sprinkle some more chilli powder on top, if liked. Chill until required.

Slimmer's tip: For an even lower-fat pâté, use quark (skimmed-milk soft cheese) instead of the cream cheese.

Simple Dried Green Pea Soup

One of the great traditional British soups is made with split green peas and still as healthy today as it has been in times past. You can add or subtract flavourings as you like, retaining the core vegetables, but green peas are very tasty au naturel and need little extra help. The peas need to be soaked overnight.

SERVES 4

- 250g/9oz dried split green peas
- 1 tbsp olive oil
- 1 onion or 2 medium leeks, chopped
- 1 medium carrot, chopped or coarsely grated
- 1.5 litres/2½ pints water or vegetable stock
- 2 sprigs fresh thyme
- 1 bay leaf
- sea salt and freshly ground black pepper

1 Cover the dried peas with lots of cold water and leave to soak overnight. Then drain and set aside.

2 Put the oil, onion or leeks and carrot into a large saucepan and stir in 2 tbsp water. Heat until sizzling, then reduce the heat, cover and cook gently for 5 minutes until softened.

3 Tip in the wet peas, then add the water or stock, herbs and some seasoning. Bring to the boil, stirring once or twice, then lower the heat to a simmer and cook, uncovered, for up to an hour until the peas break down and thicken the soup. Keep an eye on the water level, topping up with extra boiling water as necessary. Remove the woody herb stalks and the bay leaf, check the seasoning and serve.

Cook's note: A little ham or bacon is traditional in dried pea soup. This is the kind of processed meat that has been linked to cancer but a small amount eaten only occasionally will do little harm. If you decide to include some in this soup, add about 125g/4oz chopped lean organic bacon to the vegetables in step 2.

Mangetouts and Prawn Stir-fry

Mangetouts are basically just pea pods that need the briefest of cooking over a high temperature. So this is a very quick and tasty meal for one.

SERVES 1

- 100g/3½oz mangetouts, topped and tailed
- 1 tbsp oil
- 200g/7oz cooked and peeled jumbo prawns
- 3 spring onions, thickly sliced on the diagonal
- 1 fat clove garlic, thinly sliced
- 1 tbsp grated fresh root ginger or 2 tbsp ginger purée
- 2 tbsp soy sauce
- 1 tsp sesame oil
- 1 tbsp dry sherry
- ½ tsp sesame seeds
- sea salt and freshly ground black pepper

1 Heat a wok until hot, then toss in the mangetouts and oil. Quickly stir-fry for about 1 minute until the mangetouts are coated lightly in oil, turn bright green and crisp and are piping hot. Tip straight out onto a plate.

2 Reheat the wok and add the prawns, onions, garlic and ginger. Stir-fry for a good 2 minutes until piping hot, then return the mangetouts. Sprinkle in the soy sauce, sesame oil, sherry and seasoning. Toss again to coat, then tip back onto the plate. Sprinkle over the seeds and eat straight away.

Cook's note: Vegetarians can use cubes of marinated tofu instead of prawns, but make sure they are cooked until lightly crisp on the outside so they get a nice flavour.

Yellow Pea and Chicken Stew

A simple and delicious mid-week family meal – choose organic chicken thighs or diced turkey. Serve it with wholewheat pasta, brown basmati rice or small baked potatoes.

SERVES 4

- 150g/5oz dried yellow split peas, soaked, or 410g can (see notes below), drained
- 4 skinless, boneless chicken thighs, about 200g/7oz weight, or 200g/7oz lean diced turkey
- 1 onion, chopped
- 2 fat cloves garlic, crushed
- 1 medium carrot, coarsely grated
- ½ small green pepper, cored and chopped small
- 1 tbsp soy sauce
- 1 tsp dried oregano or thyme
- 400ml/14fl oz stock
- 2 tbsp chopped fresh parsley
- sea salt and freshly ground black pepper

1 If using dried peas, cover with plenty of cold water and leave overnight to soak, then drain next day and set aside.

2 Trim any fat from the chicken thighs and cut meat into small chunks. Heat a non-stick frying pan and dry fry the chicken or turkey for about 2 minutes until lightly browned. Remove to a plate with a slotted spoon.

3 Add the onion, garlic, carrot and pepper to the pan with about 2–3 tbsp water and cook, stirring, for 3–5 minutes until softened. Then return the meat and add the soy sauce, herbs, split peas, stock and seasoning to taste.

4 Bring to the boil, then cover and simmer for about 30 minutes until the peas begin to soften and break up. Keep an eye on the water level, topping up as required. Check the seasoning and serve, sprinkled with the parsley.

Cook's notes: If using canned peas, reduce the stock by a quarter and cook for 15 minutes instead of 30. Vegetarians can omit the chicken and add some nice 'meaty' mushrooms, such as fresh shitakes or chestnut buttons, instead.

Split Pea and Courgette Dhal

Indian dhal is a versatile dish – serve it as a snack, with toasted wholemeal pitta breads, or as a main course with rice and hard-boiled eggs.

SERVES 4

- 250g/9oz dried yellow split peas, or 2 x 410g cans, drained
- 1 onion, chopped
- 1 fat clove garlic, crushed
- ½ small green pepper, cored and chopped
- 1 tbsp grated fresh root ginger or 2 tbsp ginger purée
- 1 tbsp oil
- 1 tsp black mustard seeds
- 1 tsp ground turmeric
- 1 tsp mild curry powder
- 600ml/1 pint stock
- 1 medium courgette, chopped
- 2 tomatoes, chopped
- juice ½ lemon
- sea salt and freshly ground black pepper

1 If using dried peas, soak overnight in plenty of cold water to cover, then drain and set aside.

2 In a large saucepan, mix the onion, garlic, pepper and ginger with the oil, add 2 tbsp water and heat until sizzling. Turn down and cook for 2–3 minutes until softened.

3 Stir in the spices and cook for 1 minute, stirring (the mustard seeds will pop, so keep a lid handy), then mix in the peas, stock and seasoning.

4 Bring to the boil and then simmer for 20–25 minutes, stirring once or twice and topping up with a little extra water if necessary, until you have a nice soft chunky purée.

5 Add the courgettes and tomato and cook for another 5 minutes. Then stir in the lemon juice and check the seasoning.

Slimmer's tip: This is already a low-fat, low-cal dish, but to make it even lower you could omit the oil and cook the onions and flavourings in a little extra stock in step 2.

Spicy Chickpeas with Cauliflower and Spinach

Serve this with some brown basmati rice for a Middle-Eastern-style mild low-fat curry. The sauce tastes best if made with whole spices crushed in a pestle and mortar – which many of us have but probably rarely use. Otherwise use the same amount of ground spices.

SERVES 2

- 2 tsp coriander berries
- 1 tsp cumin seeds
- 3 cardamom pods
- 1 red onion, sliced
- 1 fat clove garlic, crushed
- 1 tbsp olive oil
- 1 bay leaf
- 1 small stick cinnamon
- 410g can chickpeas
- ½ small cauliflower, trimmed into about 100g/3½ small florets
- 2 tomatoes, chopped
- 150g/5oz baby leaf spinach
- sea salt and freshly ground black pepper

1 Heat the coriander and cumin in a small frying pan without oil for a few seconds until they begin to smell fragrant. Then tip into a pestle and mortar. Crack open the cardamom pods and extract the seeds, then crush with the two whole spices until finely ground.

2 Put the onion and garlic into a medium saucepan with the oil, stir to coat, then add 2 tbsp water. Heat until sizzling, then cover and sweat gently for 5 minutes.

3 Uncover and mix in the spices, plus the bay leaf and cinnamon. Cook for ½ minute, then stir in the chickpeas and the can liquor. Bring to the boil and drop in the cauliflower florets and tomatoes.

4 Season, adding extra pepper if you like a pungent spiciness, and simmer for about 5 minutes until the cauliflower is just tender, then mix in the spinach and cook until wilted. Check the seasoning and serve hot.

Steamed Sugarsnaps with Leeks and Shitakes

Sugarsnap peas (aka snowpeas) are relative newcomers to the fresh vegetable scene and brilliant for quick healthy eating because they need no preparation. They are tender peas in a pod and eaten just as they come. This is a great all-in-one vegetable dish to serve alongside fish, or in combination with another vegetable dish, or as a very low-calorie dieter's lunch. Good too with pasta or basmati rice. You will need a steamer basket to cook it.

SERVES 2

- 150g/5oz fresh shitake mushrooms, optional
- 200g/7oz sugarsnap peas
- 1 leek, thinly sliced
- 1 fat clove garlic, crushed
- 1 tbsp grated fresh root ginger or 2 tbsp ginger purée
- 1 tsp sesame oil
- 2–3 tbsp soy sauce
- 4 tbsp stock or water
- 1 tbsp balsamic vinegar
- sea salt and freshly ground black pepper

1 Trim the stalks of the shitakes, if using, as they can sometimes become a little hard, then cut into quarters or halves depending on the size.

2 Bring water to the boil in a wok or large saucepan that will take a bamboo steamer basket or metal collapsible basket.

3 Find a heatproof bowl that will fit inside the steamer basket and toss all the vegetables in it. Stir in the sesame oil, soy sauce, stock or water, vinegar and seasoning. Place the basket on the wok or pan. Cover and steam for about 4–5 minutes, by which time the vegetables should have wilted slightly.

4 Remove the lid carefully, as steam can burn. The steam and flavourings will have made a delicious, light, almost fat-free sauce.

Cook's notes: You could steam a fillet of fish on top of the vegetables at the same time. Or you could stir-fry the vegetables in a wok with 1 tbsp oil.

Slimmer's tip: Even with a fillet of white fish on top, this would still make a very low-calorie meal.

Chickpea and Sweet Potato Sauce

Perfect for pasta or spooned over baked jacket potatoes. Leftover sauce can be frozen.

SERVES 2–3

- 1 onion, chopped
- 2 fat cloves garlic, crushed
- 1 small sweet potato, peeled and chopped
- 1 tbsp olive oil
- 400g can chopped tomatoes
- 1 tbsp tomato purée
- ½ tsp dried oregano or thyme
- 410g can chickpeas, drained
- 2 tbsp chopped fresh parsley
- sea salt and freshly ground black pepper

1 Put the onion, garlic, sweet potato and oil into a saucepan and stir in 2 tbsp water. Heat until sizzling, then cover and sweat for about 5 minutes.

2 Uncover, stir in the tomatoes, purée, herbs and seasoning. Simmer for 5 more minutes, then add the chickpeas and a little water if necessary. Simmer for 5 more minutes or until the sweet potato is softened. Mix in the parsley.

Slimmer's tip: Omit the oil to lower the fat and turn this into a very low-calorie sauce. Simply simmer the vegetables in a little water for 5 minutes, then complete the recipe.

Spicy Basmati with Peas

Many rice-eating countries around the world have a version of rice with peas or beans. The two foods complement each other so well and are nutritionally perfectly balanced. The West Indians cook rice with dried peas or beans mixed with coconut and thyme, the Arabs like their rice with warm spices and lentils, while the Indians and Italians favour peas with basmati or risotto. Serve this with grilled fish or a grilled large meaty mushroom, or enjoy it with an omelette.

SERVES 2

- 250g/9oz brown basmati rice
- 1 tbsp oil
- 1 small red onion, halved and sliced
- 1 tsp cumin seeds or 2 tsp ground cumin
- 2 cardamom pods, optional
- 200g/7oz frozen peas
- sea salt and freshly ground black pepper

1 Soak the basmati in cold water to cover for 5 minutes, then rinse and drain.

2 Heat the oil in a medium-size saucepan and sauté the onion for about 3 minutes until just softened. Stir in the cumin and cook for a few seconds until the aroma is released.

3 Tip in the wet rice, add the cardamom pods, if using, 400ml/14fl oz water and ½ tsp salt. Bring to the boil, stir to separate the grains, then turn the heat right down, cover and cook for 25 minutes.

4 Uncover and gently fork through the peas, then cover and cook for another 5 minutes. Remove from the heat, still covered, and allow to sit for 5 minutes. This helps the grains to firm. Uncover, remove the cardamom pods (which should have conveniently settled on top of the rice) and fork gently through, adding extra seasoning to taste. Serve hot and steaming.

Cook's note: For a more tasty rice, use vegetable or chicken stock instead of plain water.

Slimmer's tip: To turn this into a very low-cal, low-fat dish, omit the frying (step 2) and simply mix the rice, onion and water together with the spices, bring to the boil, then simmer as above.

Peas St Germain – Peas with Braised Onions and Lettuce

This is a nice light summer dish. Ideally use very fresh, just-picked peas; otherwise a good branded pack of frozen peas will do nicely. If you can't find baby onions or shallots, use two small onions, and cut them into wedges.

SERVES 2

- 125g/4oz baby-size onions or shallots (not pickling onions)
- 1 tbsp olive oil
- 1 little gem lettuce
- 300ml/½ pint stock
- 250g/9oz podded fresh or frozen peas
- 2 tbsp reduced-fat crème fraîche, optional
- 1 tbsp chopped fresh mint
- sea salt and freshly ground black pepper

1 Dunk the onions into a pan of just boiled water and leave for 2 minutes, then drain and rinse under cold water. Peel off the skins and trim neatly around the root.

2 Place the oil in a medium-size saucepan with the onions and heat until the pan starts to sizzle. Cook on a low-medium heat until the onions start to brown lightly, about 5 minutes, stirring once or twice.

3 Meanwhile, pull off the lettuce leaves and break the larger ones in half. Cut the central core in 4 lengths. Pour the stock into the pan, bring to the boil, then drop in the lettuce and add some seasoning. Simmer for about 5 minutes until the lettuce softens; surprisingly, it holds its shape very well.

4 Add the peas and simmer for 3 more minutes, then stir in the crème fraîche, if using, and cook for 2 more minutes. Check the seasoning, sprinkle with the mint and serve.

Slimmer's tip: Omit the oil and simmer the onions in the stock for 5 minutes then proceed with the rest of the recipe. Omit the crème fraîche at the end.

6

Getting back to your roots

IF YOU THINK that all cavemen dined daily on barbecued beasts, then you have a distorted picture of primitive life. Hunting was hard then. During most periods in early societies meat was accorded cave-wall 'spin' mainly because it was an occasional treat. Hurrah, bully for us – we've managed to kill a beast! Roots, available all year round, were more common everyday fare for most of our ancestors. In fact, this situation prevailed in many societies right into the early twentieth century. The Irish starved in the potato famine of the mid nineteenth century because roots supplied around 80 per cent of their diet.

Primitive eating patterns still offer pointers to what does us good. All living creatures – even earwigs and slugs – have an inbuilt survival mechanism guiding them to their ideal diet. Unfortunately for us, this innate sense can be distorted by today's all-too-readily available foods. Our food-filled Western world constantly seduces us away from eating what comes naturally.

No need to leap back to pre-history to endorse the value of roots. Just glance back to World War Two, when we were 'digging for victory' and eating lots of them and very little in the way of animal products. Gran (better not get her started!) will gladly reminisce about root-packed, meat-free Woolton Pie. We know now that wartime Brits were much, much healthier than we are – and weighed much, much less.

Roots – especially baked potatoes, parsnips and carrots – are rich sources of good bacteria-feeding fibre, probably one of the reasons why we were healthier then. Enjoy roots more often with the recipes that follow.

BAKED POTATO MEALS

JOIN OUR CAMPAIGN to reinstate the healthy baked potato – banned by silly low-carb diets, then somewhat maligned by glycemic-index-based diets because of its relatively high GI.

Keeping blood sugar at desirably even levels depends on the GI of whole meals, not of any single ingredient. Most of all it depends on the quantity of fibre in your diet, and the F2 way of eating automatically protects you (unless you are diabetic) from blood-sugar highs and lows.

Combine baked potatoes with low-GI foods like peas and pulses, as we have in these recipes, and what you get is tasty, filling, high-fibre, low-fat (don't even think of adding butter!) meals that won't send blood-sugar levels soaring. What could be healthier?

Cook's notes

Baked potatoes are best made with floury, not waxy-fleshed spuds. Desirée, King Edwards, Marfona and Estima are good choices, depending on the season. For a normal portion, choose a medium-size potato, around 300g/10oz. Scrub if dirty (potatoes are best sold coated in earthy dirt because they keep longer), then, using the tip of a small sharp knife, score a cross on the top. For a crisp skin simply pop the potato into a medium-hot oven – 190°C/gas 5 – and cook for up to 45 minutes, testing the flesh after about 30 minutes with a thin skewer. No need to rub the skin with any oil as this only makes the skin softer. Potatoes cooked with metal skewers pushed in the centre cook faster. Alternatively, score and microwave on full power for about 10 minutes, checking after 5–6 minutes. Then allow to stand for 5 minutes before cutting open.

Fillings for baked potatoes

All recipes are sufficient for two medium-size cooked potatoes.

Curried Lentil and Onion

- 1 red onion, sliced
- 1 fat clove garlic, crushed
- 2 tsp oil
- 1 tbsp grated fresh ginger or ginger purée
- 1 tsp cumin seeds, optional
- 2 tsp mild curry powder
- 3 tbsp red split lentils or ½ x 400g can lentils
- squeeze fresh lemon juice
- 2 tbsp chopped fresh coriander or parsley
- 2 tbsp low-fat natural yogurt, to serve
- sea salt and freshly ground black pepper

1 Put the onion, garlic, oil and ginger into a saucepan and stir well to coat. Add 2 tbsp water and heat until sizzling, then cover and sweat on a low heat for 5 minutes.

2 Mix in the cumin seeds, if using, and cook for 30 seconds, then add the curry powder and cook for a few more seconds.

3 Sprinkle in the dried red lentils, if using, and a mug of water. Season well, bring to the boil, then simmer for 10–12 minutes until the lentils thicken and soften. Alternatively, add the canned lentils and cook for 5 minutes.

4 Add lemon juice to taste, check the seasoning and stir in the coriander or parsley. Spoon into the cooked potato and drizzle over the yogurt.

Cottage Cheese, Spring Onion and Corn

This is a no-cook filling.

- 250g pot low-fat cottage cheese
- 2–3 spring onions, finely chopped
- 2 tbsp chopped red pepper, or 1 fat fresh chilli, seeded and chopped
- 200g can sweetcorn, drained
- sea salt and freshly ground black pepper

1 Just mix everything together in a bowl and when the potatoes are cooked, cut open and spoon the filling inside, mounding up attractively. Use the chilli if you like a spicy kick.

Tex Mex Chilli Bean

- 1 small onion, chopped
- 1 fat clove garlic, crushed
- 2 tsp olive oil
- 1 tsp mild chilli powder
- ½ tsp ground cumin
- ½ tsp dried oregano
- 200g can chopped tomatoes
- 200g can red kidney beans, drained
- sea salt and freshly ground black pepper

1 Stir the onion, garlic and oil in a saucepan, heat until sizzling, then add 2 tbsp water, cover and sweat for 5 minutes.

2 Uncover, mix in the spices and oregano, cook for a few seconds, then tip in the tomatoes and beans, and add seasoning. Bring to the boil, then simmer for 10 minutes. Serve spooned into the centre of the potatoes.

ROOTS MAKE THE MEAL

Roots take over the starring role, rather than being a mere side issue, in these healthy fibre-rich meals.

Cook's notes

Carrots, parsnips, turnips, sweet potatoes, small sweet beetroots plus exotics such as salsify (if you ever come across any in farmers' markets) make mighty fine eating when tossed in a roasting pan with a smidgen of olive oil, smothered in herbs and spices and roasted for up to an hour. Not only do they smell wonderful during cooking and taste delicious afterwards, their colours are just so glorious that it is hard not to tuck in straight away. Naturally sweet, they can be lightly caramelized with a trickle of maple syrup or runny honey. You might also like to add some chunks of pumpkin or squash plus sliced red onions or leeks.

Roasted Red Roots

Beetroot isn't among those roots richest in fibre, but in this recipe it joins forces with and adds flavour to other roots that are. It is increasingly easy to find raw beetroot in the shops now, so if your experience of them has been restricted to jars of harsh pickled slices, you are in for a pleasant surprise. There are so many ways of enjoying beetroot, from the classic borscht soup to grating it raw in a salad with apple and nuts. By cooking the roots separately you ensure the beetroot doesn't stain everything magenta.

SERVES 4

- 1 large raw beetroot, about 500g/1lb 2oz
- 1 red onion, cut in wedges
- 2 sprigs fresh thyme
- 2–3 pinches cumin seeds
- 2 medium carrots, scrubbed and cut into bite-size chunks
- 1 large parsnip, topped and tailed and cut into bite-size chunks
- 2 tbsp balsamic vinegar
- sea salt and freshly ground black pepper

1 Heat the oven to 180°/gas 4. Tear off 2 sheets of foil about 25cm/10in square, and place them in a shallow roasting tin. Scrub the beetroot but don't peel. Trim the stalk almost to the base, leaving a little tuft sticking up.

2 Place in the middle of the foil with the onion wedges. Scatter over the leaves of 1 sprig thyme, half the cumin seeds and seasoning. Scrunch up the foil into a moneybag pouch.

3 Place the carrot and parsnip and remaining thyme, cumin and seasoning in the other foil square and scrunch into a pouch. Bake both pouches for about 35–40 minutes, or until a skewer stuck in the middle tests the roots as tender.

4 Uncover carefully to retain any juices. Cool for 10 minutes then peel the beetroot, using a pair of rubber gloves to stop your fingers staining. Cut into thick chunks and mix with the onion, carrot and parsnip chunks, pan juices and balsamic vinegar. Check the seasoning and cool to room temperature before serving.

Cook's note: You could add sticks of celery or fennel to the carrot and parsnip.

Sweet Potato and Peppers

This combination of sweet potato, red peppers, tomato and lentils makes a great vegetarian main meal – perfect to serve with wholewheat pasta or brown basmati rice.

SERVES 4

- 2 sweet potatoes, about 600g/1lb 4oz total weight
- 1 red pepper, cored and chopped
- 1 onion, chopped
- 1 fat clove garlic, crushed
- 1 tbsp olive oil
- 1 x 400g can chopped tomatoes
- 3 tbsp red lentils
- ½ tsp dried oregano
- sea salt and freshly ground black pepper

1 Peel the sweet potato and cut into small chunks. Place in a saucepan with the pepper, onion, garlic, oil and 2–3 tbsp water. Heat until sizzling then cover and cook gently for about 5 minutes until softened.

2 Uncover, add the tomatoes, lentils, oregano and 300ml (½ pint) water. Season, bring to the boil then simmer gently for 15 minutes until the lentils have thickened and the potato is soft. Check the seasoning and serve.

Cook's note: Sweet potato makes marvellous mash on its own. Simply boil in the same way as for normal potatoes for 10–12 minutes, then drain (saving a small cup of the cooking water) and mash, adding a little of the water and a small knob of olive spread or a trickle of olive oil to make it creamy. Season with some freshly grated nutmeg, salt and pepper. This goes well with grilled chicken, Christmas turkey or oily fish like salmon.

BBQ Roots with Pesto Dressing

Barbecues can be mildly depressing occasions for vegetarians unless some inspired host adds slices of root vegetables to the grill. Thick slices of sweet potato and carrots, halved lengthways, with rounds of onions or shallots and maybe a couple of large portabello mushrooms, make for a tempting selection. But don't restrict this dish to the vegetarians; it is so tasty everyone will be queuing for a share.

SERVES 4

- 1 large sweet potato, thinly peeled and cut in thick slices
- 2 medium carrots, halved lengthways
- 4 shallots, peeled, or 1 onion in 4 slices
- 1 tbsp pesto
- 2–3 tbsp Light Vinaigrette, page 68
- a few leaves fresh basil, roughly torn
- sea salt and freshly ground black pepper

1 Heat the BBQ until it dies down to an ashy glow – not too hot and flaming or you will burn the food.

2 Lay the sweet potato and carrots straight onto the rack. Note – no oil, as this will cause a flare-up. Lay the shallots or onion slices alongside and cook them all, turning a few times to stop them burning. Check when they are cooked and move to a platter, season lightly, and cover loosely with foil so the steam moistens the food a little.

3 When they are all cooked, mix together the pesto and vinaigrette and drizzle over. Toss over the torn basil and serve at room temperature.

7

Greens – the pick of the crop

T HOUGH ALL GREENS are helpfully low in calories, there's a big variation in the bio benefits they provide. On the one hand there are the so-so sort of greens – the lettuce and cucumber lot – which, being mainly water, contain only small, dilute quantities of bacteria-feeding fibre, vitamins and minerals. Then there are the go-for-it greens, rich sources of both. Among the latter, apart from those already mentioned such as leeks and peas, are the sprouts, broccoli, spinach and cabbage featured in the following recipes.

Cook's notes

These days growers are quite ingenious in tempting us to eat up our greens, with new varieties like unusual forms of broccoli, or baby-size cabbages, the light crisp pointed cabbage and crinkly Savoys. Sprouts, often thought of as a winter-only vegetable, can now be eaten throughout the year. Spinach is sold washed, spun dry and ready bagged. The most tender are the baby-leaf varieties, perfect for salads and stir-fries, while larger leaves with stalks are best for steaming or light simmering. Neither needs more than a splash or two of cooking water and should be well drained after cooking, pressing down gently with the back of a big spoon in the colander or sieve.

If you prefer to use frozen spinach or sprouts (which are just as high in vitamins as fresh), cook them from frozen for the shortest possible time.

Brussels Sprout and Turkey Stir-fry

Although this dish is perfect for using up leftover cooked meat after the festive feast, the combination of sprouts and turkey is perfect whatever the time of year. You do need to make sure the shredded turkey is piping hot when serving.

SERVES 4

- 400–500g/14oz–1lb 2oz trimmed sprouts
- 300–400g/10–14oz cooked organic turkey meat
- 1 red onion, halved then thinly sliced into half moons
- 1 fat clove garlic, crushed
- 1–2 tbsp freshly grated root ginger
- 1 tbsp olive oil
- 1 tsp Chinese Five Spice powder, optional
- 1 medium carrot, coarsely grated
- 1 tbsp sesame seeds or 2 tbsp toasted flaked almonds
- 1 large spring onion, slit lengthways and shredded

SAUCE

- 2–3 tbsp soy sauce
- 2 tsp cornflour
- 2 tbsp dry sherry
- 1 tsp sesame oil
- 1 tsp clear honey

1 Cut the sprouts into halves or quarters, depending on their size. Remove any fat and skin from the turkey and pull into long thin shreds.

2 Mix the onion, garlic and ginger with the oil in a wok and heat until it starts to sizzle, stirring once or twice. Cook for about 2 minutes.

3 Then mix in the Five Spice powder, if using, and cook for 1 minute. Add the sprouts, and pour in about 100ml/3½ fl oz water with some seasoning. Bring to the boil, stirring well, and cook on a medium heat for around 2 minutes until the sprouts start to soften.

4 Mix in the carrot and shredded turkey and cook for 2 more minutes. By this time the liquid should have reduced right down.

5 Meanwhile, mix the sauce ingredients in a cup with 2 tbsp water and toss into the pan, stirring until it thickens. Reheat well until the turkey is piping hot. Sprinkle with the sesame seeds or almonds and serve immediately, garnished with the spring onion shreds.

Slimmer's tip: You can omit the pre-frying of the onion, etc., by tossing them in a hot wok or pan and adding splashes of water.

Sprouting Broccoli with Crispy Garlic and Anchovy

Slender stems of purple sprouting or tender sweet broccoli are a delicious variation on the tight heads of broccoli. They are sold ready trimmed – goodness in an instant. Instead of boiling, cook them in a wok with a little oil and water and topped with slivers of toasted garlic and anchovies, which melt in the pan as a piquant sauce. Served with wholewheat pasta or boiled basmati rice, this makes a light and healthy meal.

SERVES 2
- 1 fat clove garlic
- about 6 anchovy fillets
- 2–3 spring onions
- 1 tbsp olive oil
- 250g pack purple sprouting or tender sweet broccoli
- freshly ground black pepper

1 Slice the garlic wafer-thin on the diagonal. Pat the anchovies dry of oil and snip into small pieces. Slice the onions on the diagonal.

2 Heat half the oil in a non-stick frying pan or wok and sprinkle in the garlic, stirring gently until it turns light brown and crisp. Remove to a paper towel.

3 Add the remaining oil and 3 tbsp water. Toss in the broccoli and cook for about 3 minutes, stirring often until the stems begin to soften, and adding extra splashes of water if necessary. Scatter over the anchovies and mix in and grind over pepper to taste. No salt, because of the anchovies.

4 When the anchovies start to dissolve, add the onions and mix in. By now the broccoli stems will be just tender. Serve with the garlic sprinkled over.

Pistou – Provençal Cabbage and Bean Soup with Basil Purée

Cabbage is an excellent year-round vegetable, as this sunny Mediterranean main-meal soup shows. Drizzle it just before serving with fresh basil purée. This makes an ideal low-fat, low-cal meal for dieters.

SERVES 4
- 1 medium potato, scrubbed and chopped small
- 1 carrot, chopped small
- 1 leek, thinly sliced
- 1 small red or white onion, chopped
- 2 cloves garlic, crushed
- 1 tbsp olive oil
- ½ x 420g can cannellini beans or 125g cooked haricot beans
- 1.5 litres/2½ pints stock
- ½ small Savoy or other green cabbage
- 2 plum tomatoes, skinned and cut into chunks
- about 6 sprigs fresh basil
- sea salt and freshly ground black pepper

1 Put the potato, carrot, leek, onion and garlic into a large saucepan with the oil and 3 tbsp water. Heat until sizzling, then cover and sweat for 5 minutes.

2 Uncover, add the beans, stock and seasoning to taste. Bring to the boil and simmer for 10 minutes.

3 Meanwhile, cut the cabbage half into 2 quarters and cut out the core. Then using a sharp, long-bladed knife, shred the cabbage as finely as possible. Bring a pan of water to the boil and toss in the cabbage. Boil for 1 minute until just wilted, then drain into a colander and run under cold water so it becomes bright green. Shake well to drain.

4 Add the tomato chunks to the soup and lightly cook for 2–3 minutes. In the meantime, tear the basil sprigs, including the thinner stalks, into a blender and whiz to a purée, adding about 2–3 tbsp water to thin down. Scrape out into a cup.

5 When ready to serve, check the seasoning of the soup and stir in the bright green cabbage. Reheat until boiling then immediately ladle into warm bowls and drizzle on the basil sauce.

Cook's note: You could leave out the blanching of the cabbage and simply toss the shreds into the simmering soup along with the tomatoes, but the cabbage does taste nicer for the blanching, looks brighter and adds a certain finesse to this classic dish.

Fish with Creamy Cabbage

Cabbage and fish may sound a surprising combination, but it works well. Cooked with shallots or onions and carrots, the mixture is moist enough not to require a separate sauce.

SERVES 2

- 2 x 125g/4oz fillets cod or salmon, skin on
- ½ small green cabbage, about 300g/10oz, preferably Savoy
- 1 large shallot or small onion, thinly sliced
- 1 medium carrot, cut into julienne (thin) sticks
- 1 tbsp olive oil
- leaves from 1 sprig fresh thyme or marjoram
- about 100ml/3fl oz stock or water
- 3–4 tbsp fat-free fromage frais
- 2 tbsp chopped parsley
- 2 wedges fresh lemon, to garnish
- sea salt and freshly ground black pepper

1 Preheat the oven to 190°C/gas 5. Season the fish, cover loosely with a little foil and bake for about 10 minutes until just firm. Then continue cooking for another 5 minutes or so. Remove and set aside.

2 Meanwhile, cut the cabbage half into 2 quarters and cut out the core. Then using a sharp, long-bladed knife, shred the cabbage as finely as possible.

3 Mix the onion and carrot in a large saucepan and stir in the oil. Heat until sizzling, add the herbs, some seasoning and 3 tbsp water, cover and cook for 3 minutes. Pour in the stock and add the cabbage. Reheat to boiling, stirring frequently to keep the cabbage shreds moving so they cook evenly. After about 3 minutes they will begin to wilt.

4 Take off the heat, stir in the fromage frais and reheat slightly until hot, but do not allow to boil. Stir in the parsley. Divide the cabbage between two warm plates and place the fish on top. Garnish with the lemon wedges and more black pepper.

Cook's note: The cabbage shreds should be quite crisp when served, so make and serve this dish without much hanging around. The vegetable mix goes well as an accompaniment for other meals as well, not just fish.

Velvety Broccoli Soup

Sometimes the fewer ingredients in a dish, the more sublime the flavour. This is certainly true of this soup, which is really just liquefied broccoli that not only tastes wonderful but has a beautiful bright green colour. Serve with a swirl of low-fat natural yogurt.

SERVES 4
- 1kg/2lb 4oz broccoli florets only, no stalks
- 125g/4oz quark or reduced-fat crème fraîche
- sea salt and freshly ground black pepper

1 Chop the broccoli so the florets are all the same size. Pour 1.5 litres/2½ pints water into a saucepan with 1 tbsp salt and bring to the boil.

2 Toss in the broccoli, return to the boil, then simmer for 8–10 minutes until tender. Strain off the water into a jug and save it.

3 Whiz the florets in a food processor for what seems like an inordinate length of time: at least 2 minutes, scraping down the sides once or twice. This stage is necessary so you get a really smooth purée.

4 With the machine running, slowly pour the saved cooking water back into the processor. Stop when the liquid is silky and the consistency of single cream. It should not be watery. Then add half the quark or crème fraîche, seasoning to taste, and whiz to blend for a few seconds.

5 Reheat to serve, swirled with either quark (which has been thinned a little with warm water) or the crème fraîche.

Cook's note: You could add a sliced leek to the pan in step 2 for extra flavour.

Spinach Salad with Croûtons

Baby leaf spinach is sold ready washed and spun, in convenient bags enough for two servings. So all you have to do is gather together some delicious and healthy ingredients to go with it, such as herby croûtons, mushrooms and some thin slivers of red pepper, tossed together with a little vinaigrette dressing.

SERVES 2

- 200g bag baby leaf spinach
- 125g/4oz Low-fat Oven Croûtons, page 159
- ½ red pepper, cored and thinly sliced
- 125g/4oz button mushrooms, thinly sliced
- 3–4 tbsp Light Vinaigrette, page 68
- 1–2 tbsp balsamic vinegar
- sea salt and freshly ground black pepper

1 Pick over the spinach leaves and discard any that look past their best. Tip into a big salad bowl.

2 Add the croûtons, pepper strips, mushrooms and seasoning to the spinach bowl.

3 Pour over the vinaigrette and toss together, making sure everything is well coated. Divide between two shallow bowls, drizzle with the vinegar and serve.

Slimmer's tip: If you want to cut calories further, increase the balsamic vinegar to 2 tbsp per serving and cut back on the vinaigrette.

Spinach and Mushroom Pilaff

This dish is basically a simple brown-rice pilaff into which you stir mushrooms and spinach just before serving. Serve sprinkled with toasted pinenuts or flaked almonds.

SERVES 2

- 180g/6oz brown basmati rice
- 1 onion, finely chopped
- 1 fat clove garlic, crushed
- 1 tbsp olive oil
- 1 tsp ground cumin or mild curry powder
- 450ml/15fl oz stock or water, plus extra for mushrooms
- 180g/6oz button mushrooms, sliced
- 200g bag baby leaf spinach
- sea salt and freshly ground black pepper

1 Rinse the basmati in a large bowl of cold water, swishing the grains with your hand, then tip out the water, leaving the rice behind in the bottom of the bowl. Fill with cold water again and leave for 5 minutes, then drain in a sieve.

2 Mix the onion and garlic in a large pan with the oil. Heat until sizzling, add 2 tbsp water, then cover and simmer gently for 3 minutes.

3 Uncover and mix in the spice. Cook for ½ minute longer, then stir in the rice, pour in the stock or water, and season.

4 Bring to the boil, then clamp on the lid and turn the heat down to low. Cook gently for around 20–25 minutes until the grains are just tender.

5 Meanwhile, simmer the mushrooms in another pan in a little more stock and seasoning for about 5 minutes, stirring once or twice. Mix into the rice with a fork and then add the spinach, cooking until it too begins to wilt. Reheat until piping hot and serve.

Creamed Sprouts and Leeks

Sprouts can develop a particular aroma if cooked ahead and kept warm. One way round this is to cool them immediately after boiling under cold running water, then whiz into a purée with nutmeg and a low-fat natural yogurt or fromage frais. This is delicious served with almost any other dish.

SERVES 4

- 500g/1lb 2oz fresh even-sized Brussels sprouts
- 2 medium leeks, washed and chopped
- a little freshly grated nutmeg
- 3 tbsp fat-free fromage frais
- 1–2 tbsp chopped fresh parsley
- sea salt and freshly ground black pepper

1 Trim the stalks of the sprouts and peel off any discoloured outer leaves.

2 Bring a large pan of water to the boil and add 2 tsp salt. Toss in the sprouts and leeks and boil for 3–5 minutes until just tender with a slight crisp edge. Drain, reserving about a cup of the cooking liquid, then hold the vegetables in the colander under a cold running tap until cold.

3 Shake dry and tip into a food processor. Whiz to a chunky purée, using the pulse button to control it, season with the nutmeg to taste (but not too much as excess nutmeg can taste bitter), then dollop in the fromage frais. Whiz just enough to blend, adding a little of the saved water if it is too thick. It should be creamy and spoonable.

4 Check the seasoning, add half the parsley and whiz for a few seconds to blend. Scrape into a heatproof dish. When ready to serve, reheat gently in a microwave until piping hot and sprinkle over parsley to serve.

8

The fast-forward fibre

THE TOTAL AMOUNT of fibre was once considered all that really counted in ensuring its health benefits. Diversity is now known to be an equally important factor. Different forms of fibre from different foods impact in different ways, interacting to fully mobilize your protective inner army.

Wheat fibre doesn't actually feed good bacteria. But it helps them get sufficient of the fibre that does.

Think of it as 'the fast-forward fibre'. It speeds potentially toxic waste-matter through the gut, a crucial process when you know that half the British population has a dangerously slow transit time. (Enough said about matters lavatorial in a cookery book – but you have been warned!) At the same time it pushes bacteria-feeding fibre to the far end of the gut, where it is in short supply, enabling good bacteria to extend their essential protective functions.

Rye and corn fibres share this benefit, but it's difficult to eat them in the quantity required. There isn't much fibre in corn-based cereals. Oats have bacteria-feeding benefits but lack this fast-forward function. Wheat fibre, on the other hand, is widely and richly available in a variety of foods. These recipes can help fast-forward you on the route to positive health.

Sweet yet low

Contrary to a common misconception, the fat content of many sweet dishes is a much greater threat than the sugar. When the two partner up, as they do in most cakes, biscuits and puds, the fat accounts for most of the calories and – when saturated or hydrogenated – the cholesterol-raising impact.

A little sugar will do little harm if combined with healthy ingredients. It is when large quantities are downed 'neat' – as in the case of sugary canned drinks – that they provide empty and often surplus calories.

On the following pages we've lowered the fat content, chosen healthier fats and combined sugar with wheat fibre to provide much healthier versions of two favourite sweet treats.

Healthy wheaty extras

Sprinkle on the croûtons or grate on the cheese and you risk adding so many fatty calories to a dish. Here are tasty alternatives, which add fibre and reduce fat.

Herby Wholemeal Topping Crumbs

Oven-dried crumbs sprinkled on top of baked vegetable dishes or over pasta meals make a good very low-fat alternative to grated cheese. Again, leftover wholemeal bread (around 3–4 days old) can be used for this. Make as much as you want and store in the fridge ready for shaking on top of meals. The herbs can be left out if you prefer.

MAKES ENOUGH TO FILL A LARGE JAM JAR
- 4–6 slices wholemeal bread
- 1 tsp dried mixed herbs
- freshly ground black pepper

1 Heat the oven to the low setting. Place the bread directly on the oven shelves and bake for up to 2 hours until very brittle and dry.

2 Cool, then whiz in a food processor or blender to fine crumbs. Add the herbs and pepper for a few seconds, then tip into a food container or jam jar.

Low-fat Oven Croûtons

If you have leftover wholemeal bread a few days old, don't waste it. Give it a new lease of life as oven-crisped, low-fat croûtons. Serve sprinkled on soup or in salad.

SERVES 4

- 3–4 slices wholemeal bread
- 1 tbsp olive oil
- 1 tsp dried mixed herbs
- 1 tsp crushed sea salt
- freshly ground black pepper

1 Cut the crusts from the bread, then cut into small cubes, about 1cm/½in. Pop into a large food bag and trickle in the oil.

2 Twist the bag to seal and shake well, rubbing the bread cubes gently together so they all get a very thin film of oil. Add the herbs and seasoning, then shake out the cubes in a single layer onto a shallow roasting tin.

3 Heat the oven to 150°C/gas 2 and bake for about 45 minutes until crisp, turning once or twice. Remove and cool then bag and seal until required. Store in the fridge for up to 2 weeks.

Wholewheat pasta meals

Next to high-fibre breakfast cereals, wholewheat pasta is one of the richest sources of fast-forward fibre. Cold pasta salads, which have the added bonus of resistant starch, can be found on pages 60–62. But, eaten hot, wholewheat pasta still offers major health benefits. Make more of it in your menus with the recipes below.

Cook's notes

Wholewheat pasta has a nice, slightly grainy texture. You can find it as macaroni, spaghetti or shapes such as shells or fusilli twists. It needs a few extra minutes' boiling time than white-flour pasta. The Italians often serve their pasta still slightly wet, not overdrained, which uses less oil or sauce to serve. You can save a cup of the cooking water when you drain the pasta to add to the sauce. For extra flavour, toss the pasta in a little crushed raw garlic and lots of chopped fresh parsley before mixing with the sauce. Allow 50–75g uncooked pasta per head and cook it while you make the sauce of your choice.

Macaroni, Tuna & Broccoli Bake

This makes a nice all-in-one homely meal.

SERVES 2

- 150g/5oz wholewheat macaroni or wholewheat pasta shapes
- 1 onion, red or white, chopped
- 1 head broccoli, broken in small florets
- 300ml/½ pint semi-skimmed milk
- 1 tbsp cornflour
- ½ tsp dried mixed herbs
- 1 x 200g can tuna in brine or spring water
- 1 x 200g can sweetcorn, optional, drained
- 3–4 tbsp Herby Wholemeal Topping Crumbs, page 158

1 Cook the macaroni or pasta shapes with the chopped onion in plenty of salted boiling water according to pack instructions, about 12–15 minutes. Add the broccoli florets for the last 2 minutes. Drain, tip into a shallow ovenproof dish and set aside.

2 Stir 2–3 tbsp milk in a cup with the cornflour to a paste. Put the remainder of the milk into the saucepan and bring to boil. Tip a little hot milk into the cup of cornflour paste and stir briskly then pour this back into the pan, stirring until thickened. Season nicely and add the herbs.

3 Drain the tuna and flake in the tin with a fork, then stir gently into the sauce along with the corn, if using. Reheat until just bubbling and pour it over the pasta and vegetables. Sprinkle the top with crumbs. Preheat the grill and brown the topping until crisp and golden.

Salmon, Leek and Spinach Pasta

Nice with wholewheat fusilli twists. Put them on to cook while you make this sauce. To boost the flavour, add some strips of smoked salmon just before serving.

SERVES 2

- 2 salmon steaks, about 100g/3½oz each
- 1 leek, thinly sliced
- 1 tbsp olive oil
- 1 fat clove garlic, crushed
- 2 tbsp dry vermouth or 4 tbsp dry white wine, optional
- 3 tbsp reduced-fat crème fraîche and a small cup of pasta cooking water
- 2 good handfuls baby leaf spinach, about 125g/4oz
- about 50g/2oz smoked salmon, cut in strips, optional
- sea salt and freshly ground black pepper

1 Skin the salmon by running a sharp knife between the skin and flesh, then cut the flesh into small bite-size cubes. Check for any bones.

2 Mix the leek, oil and garlic in a saucepan and heat until they start to sizzle. Add 3 tbsp water, cover and cook on a low heat for about 3 minutes until softened.

3 Add the vermouth or wine, if using, and cook until evaporated. Toss in the salmon cubes and cook for about 2 minutes without stirring until lightly done.

4 Season, then turn the cubes and cook for another minute. Gently mix in the crème fraîche and enough pasta cooking water to make a thin creamy sauce.

5 Add the spinach, stirring gently until wilted, and the smoked salmon strips, if using, then check the seasoning. When the pasta is cooked, drain and either toss into the salmon sauce or spoon the sauce on top.

Greek Salad and Cottage Cheese

If you've been on holiday to Greece you will remember the wonderful fresh tomato, cucumber and feta cheese salads that appear at almost every meal. This filling is inspired by that combination of foods, except instead of high fat and salty feta, we suggest using cottage cheese. Add a few sliced black olives, too, if you feel in a Mediterranean mood, and swap the mint for coriander sprigs if you prefer.

SERVES 2

- 5cm/2in piece cucumber
- 1–2 tomatoes
- 200g tub low-fat natural cottage cheese
- 1 tbsp shredded or chopped fresh mint
- 2 wholemeal pittas or 4 slices grainy bread
- 6 pitted black olives, sliced, optional
- sea salt and freshly ground black pepper

1 Halve the cucumber and slice thinly into half moons. Do the same with the tomatoes.

2 Mix the cottage cheese with seasoning and the mint.

3 Slit open the pittas, if using. Spoon a little cheese into the pittas or spread on half the bread. Top with the cucumber and tomatoes and season lightly again. Scatter over the olives, if using, wrap and set aside until required.

Smoked Mackerel, Onion and Soft Cheese

Small fillets of smoked mackerel are easily available in supermarkets, each fillet enough for one serving. They keep well in the fridge. But go easy on the quantity if you are trying to shed weight. Although the oil is of the healthy kind – a source of omega 3 – mackerel contains a large quantity, making it high in calories.

SERVES 2

- 2 fillets smoked mackerel, ideally coated in coarse black pepper, about 100g each
- 2 spring onions, chopped
- 1 tomato, chopped
- 2 tbsp extra light Philadelphia soft cheese (5 per cent fat)
- squeeze fresh lemon juice
- 2 thick slices wholemeal bread, or baps sliced in half
- sea salt and freshly ground black pepper

1 Skin and flake the mackerel into a bowl. Check for any stray bones. Flake with a fork and mix with the onion and tomato.

2 Soften the cheese with a fork until smooth, then stir gently into the mackerel mix. Check for seasoning and add lemon juice to taste.

3 Toast the bread slices or grill the split baps and pile the mackerel on top. Serve immediately.

9

High-
fibre
fruits

FRUIT FIBRE FEEDS good bacteria in the gut, helps lower bad cholesterol in the blood and offers a multitude of health benefits. You get very valuable cancer-preventive vitamins as well as fibre from fruits such as citrus fruits and berries. And acidic citrus fruits have special value in keeping blood-sugar levels on a desirably even keel.

Among the best bioactive fruits are all the berries – raspberries, blackberries, strawberries, blueberries. The most common everyday fruits, apples, oranges and pears, are also rich sources of fruit fibre. Cherries, kiwi fruit, plums and peaches are good too. On the whole it is better to eat fruit than drink fruit in the form of juice, because this way you get the fibre too. But if you don't have weight worries (a glass of fruit juice can add up to quite a lot of calories), it's fine to do both. The following delicious fruity desserts are our way of tempting you to enjoy more fruit.

Slimmer's tips

Sugar supplies only half the calories of fat. It is only when it is combined with fat, as it is in so many foods – cakes, biscuits, ice cream, etc. – or swigged down in canned drinks (which do nothing to satisfy the appetite) that it becomes a major culprit in weight gains. Otherwise, used in moderation, it doesn't really deserve its bad reputation. Nor does it compare with saturated and hydrogenated fats as a threat to health.

However, when you are trying to lose weight and every calorie counts, you can add a touch of sweetness to prepared fruit with icing sugar. It tastes sweeter because it dissolves more quickly on the tongue. Fructose (fruit sugar) also tastes sweeter than sucrose (ordinary sugar) so you can use about a third less. The new low-calorie sugar-based sweeteners can be sprinkled over to taste and can be used for cooking.

Fruits of the Forest Mousse

This light fruity mousse is best made with home-produced berries at the peak of the season – good value and full of flavour.

SERVES 4

- 125g/4oz ripe strawberries
- 150g/5oz raspberries
- 100g/3 ½oz blueberries
- 2 tbsp caster sugar, or fructose or artificial sweetener to taste
- 200g tub fat-free fromage frais
- 2 tsp gelatine crystals
- 2 free-range egg whites
- squeeze fresh lemon juice

1 Reserve 2 of the prettiest strawberries and save a few raspberries and blueberries for serving. Toss the others into a food processor with the sugar or sweetener to taste. Whiz to a pulp, tip into a big bowl and mix in the fromage frais.

2 Pour 2 tbsp cold water into a cup then sprinkle over the gelatine. Leave until it absorbs water like wet sand. Then place the cup either in a small pan of simmering water until the gelatine melts or heat in a microwave oven on the defrost setting until the liquid turns clear – don't allow to overheat. Remove and cool for a few minutes.

3 Beat 2–3 tbsp berry mix into the gelatine, then stir this briskly into the remaining berry mix. Leave to cool and partially set.

4 Whisk the egg whites with a squeeze of lemon juice until they form firm but not dry peaks. Fold this into the berry mix and spoon into four pretty glasses. Chill until set. Halve the strawberries and use with the saved berries to decorate the mousses.

Cook's note: Use natural low-fat or flavoured yogurt if you can't find fat-free fromage frais. Elderly or pregnant women should take care with uncooked egg whites.

Rhubarb and Strawberry Fool

In the mid-winter, slender stems of pretty pink rhubarb appear on the fruit counters. Instead of making high-fat crumbles, try a high-fibre fool, mixing them with some crushed strawberries and creamy, fat-free quark. Serve with a ratafia or digestive biscuit.

SERVES 4
- 400g pack pink rhubarb, trimmed and chopped
- 50g/2oz caster sugar or 40g/1½oz fructose
- 1 tsp vanilla essence
- 250g tub quark
- 125g/4oz ripe strawberries
- 4 ratafia or digestive biscuits, optional

1 Wash the rhubarb and shake dry, then place in a saucepan with the sugar or fructose (or a low-cal sweetener) and vanilla. Heat until sizzling, then cover and turn the heat right down. No need to add extra water.

2 Cook for about 10 minutes until the fruit is tender. Remove and strain off the juice into a jug. Tip the fruit into a bowl. Return the juice to the pan and boil down until syrupy and reduced by half. Mix this with the quark to loosen it.

3 Crush the strawberries with a fork to a rough purée and mix into the rhubarb, followed by the quark, stirring loosely so you get a marbled effect. Spoon into 4 glasses and chill until ready to serve. Accompany by the biscuits, which can be crushed over the top, if liked.

Cook's note: Out of the rhubarb season, use crushed raspberries.

Yogurt Pannacotta with Crushed Mixed Berries

Pannacotta is a high-fat dessert made with cream or mascarpone, but it is possible to make a low-fat version using flavoured yogurt. The velvety texture is the same and it looks almost identical on a plate. For a special treat mix in some real vanilla seeds and serve with a crushed berry salad.

SERVES 4

- 2 tsp gelatine crystals
- 1 vanilla pod or 1 tsp vanilla extract
- 500g pot low-fat lemon yogurt
- 100g/3½oz blueberries
- 100g/3½oz raspberries
- 100g/3½oz strawberries
- sugar, fructose or low-calorie sweetener to taste

1 Put 2 tbsp cold water into a cup and stir in the gelatine. Leave until it begins to look like wet sand, then dissolve by placing the cup in a pan of gently simmering water or in a microwave on the defrost setting for a minute or two. When clear, set aside for a few moments.

2 Meanwhile, slit the vanilla pod, if using, down the middle with a thin sharp knife and using the tip scrape out the tiny sticky seeds. Put the yogurt into a big bowl and mix in the vanilla seeds, or if using extract then simply stir it in.

3 Spoon 2 tbsp yogurt into the cup of dissolved gelatine, then mix this into the rest of the yogurt. Divide between 4 small pudding moulds or ramekin dishes and chill to set.

(continued on p. 186)

4 Mix the fruits in a bowl and crush with a fork, adding sugar, fructose or sweetener to taste.

5 When the pannacottas have set, run a table knife round the edge and shake out onto small dessert plates. Spoon the fruit crush on top and serve.

Cook's notes: You could vary the flavoured yogurt. Or use reduced-fat Greek-style yogurt flavoured with honey and cinnamon. Serve with baby seedless red grapes.

Orange and Lemon Salad

Ordinary oranges can taste quite special when you take the trouble to peel and serve them properly. They are perhaps nicest served very simply dressed with lemon juice and grated zest and possibly some chopped mint. When you prepare fresh oranges, don't remove the inner membranes as they contain valuable fibre. You could substitute a pink grapefruit for one or two of the oranges.

SERVES 2
- 1 lemon
- 3 large seedless oranges, such as navels
- a little caster or icing sugar, to taste
- 1–2 tbsp chopped fresh mint

1 Finely grate the zest from the lemon and squeeze the juice. Set aside.

2 Using a sharp thin-bladed or serrated knife, slice the top and bottom off an orange then place it flat on a board. Slice off the peel, cutting from top to bottom. Repeat all the way around until you have a ball of orange. Cut this in 5mm/¼in rounds, then into halves or quarters. Scrape into a bowl along with any juice and sprinkle with a little sugar, fructose or sweetener to taste, plus some lemon zest and lemon juice.

3 Repeat with the remaining oranges, sweetener and juice. Scatter over the mint, cover and chill until required.

Blackberry, Apple and Pear Brown Betty

Here is a lighter version of a great British favourite hot pudding, using cubes of wholemeal bread for a light crunchy topping.

SERVES 4

- 1 Granny Smith apple, cored and chopped
- 1 Conference pear, cored and chopped
- 250g/9oz blackberries
- 2 slices wholemeal bread, about 100g/3½oz
- 1 tbsp low-fat spread
- 1 tbsp demerara sugar
- ½ tsp ground cinnamon

1 Put the chopped fruit and berries into a saucepan and add a splash of water. Heat until sizzling, then cover and simmer the fruit gently for about 5 minutes until the juices start to run and the fruit is par-cooked. Tip into a medium-size ovenproof dish.

2 Cut the crusts from the bread, then cut the bread into small 1cm/½in cubes. Melt the low-fat spread in a saucepan and mix in the bread until well coated. Spoon over the fruit and sprinkle with the sugar and cinnamon.

3 Heat the oven to 190°C/gas 5 and bake for about 20 minutes until browned and crisp on top. Cool for 10 minutes, then serve.

Cook's notes: You can vary the fruits according to season. Raspberries and blueberries are perfect either with or instead of the blackberries. A sliced greenish banana would add health-beneficial resistant starch.

INDEX